Fables for God's People

※

F·A·B·L·E·S
For God's People

——— ❋ ———

JOHN R. AURELIO

❋ ❋ ❋

CROSSROAD · NEW YORK

1993
The Crossroad Publishing Company
370 Lexington Avenue, New York, N.Y. 10017

Printed in the United States of America

Library of Congress Cataloging in Publication Data

Aurelio, John.
  Fables for God's people.

  1. Fables, American.   I. Title.
PS3551.U76F33   1988   813'.54   87-22154
ISBN 0-8245-0861-0 (pbk.)

To the simple whom God has chosen
to confound the wise

Contents

※

Foreword

※

Over the years I have come to learn that there are two types of fables—those for children and those for the child-hearted (never to be mistaken for the childish of either category). However, the true heart of a fable is an adult fruit.

To reduce the profound to the simple is no easy task. Few accomplish it with grace and precision. Aesop was a master at it. A master, I might add, without equal. To bear the fruit of adult experience in simple language *and* in a short story is his legendary legacy. Only the truly brave (or foolish) would attempt to walk in his footsteps.

What I have written are fables for the child-hearted. There are depths and nuances in adult language that I found too difficult to express in child-words. I ask the children to forgive me for this shortcoming. I humbly offer this work as a feeble attempt to sequel the master. If the art or the grace is not there, I can only say that my heart is.

Fables for God's People

※

The Artisan's Apprentice

※

Once there was a great artisan whose fame and renown were known the world over. Because he was very old it was rumored that he would take on only one more apprentice. Since it was a prize greatly to be sought after, to be the great man's last apprentice, regional contests were held so as to send him only the best that they had to offer. When the eliminations were at last over, three young men stood at the great Master's door.

"Make me a cup," he said, and left.

The three set about their task with all the power and talent and knowledge at their disposal. Allesandro was every bit the fine product of the wealthy class he represented. His work was always meticulously planned, richly and delicately ornamented, and patiently crafted. Massimo, on the other hand, dealt best in power and strength. His was a talent honed from the merchant class, and the beauty of his work lay in its practicality and durability. And the third apprentice, like the masses he came from, bore neither a distinguishable talent nor a memorable name. He was aptly called Poverino.

Each set about his task with singleness of purpose and would gladly have worked without stopping until the labor was done were it not for the Master's wife. She was big and bossy, as befitted her size. But she, too, had her task: to feed, house, clothe, and, in short, provide for all the needs of those under her care. Whether willingly or reluctantly, they all shared in her work unavoidably. The Master, quietly; Allesandro, fussingly and quickly; Massimo, expansively; and Poverino, endlessly.

When at long last, or far too quickly, their novitiate had come to an end, the three cups were placed on a table for the Master's choice and the world's approval.

Allessandro's chalice was unquestionably a work of rare beauty. It was so delicately thin that it was almost transparent. And yet etched ever so finely on the circumference of the cup were exquisite figures of magnificently plumed birds amid an array of infinitely detailed wildflowers. The colors were so gentle and so amazingly real that the cup seemed more the result of a wizard's magic than a craftsman's labor.

Massimo's cup, on the other hand, was more urn than cup. Yet here, too, there was a powerful beauty to the work. It was massive in size, conveying a warm and comfortable sense of strength and endurance. What it may have lacked in gentility, it more than compensated for in stability.

Poverino's cup was nothing more or less than that—a cup. Neither delicately beautiful nor imposingly strong, it could at best only be described as functional. In truth, one could justifiably wonder how he had come so far with so little talent.

There was an air of hushed expectancy when the great Master entered the room. He carefully examined each of

Little Breath

※

Once upon a time there was a little breath. He lived in the air. He moved freely and easily anywhere and everywhere he wanted to go. It was wonderful and exhilarating.

Then one day Little Breath said to the air, "I want to know who I am and where I am."

"I know who you are and where you are all the time," said the air.

"But I want to be able to tell me from you. I want . . . a . . . a . . . " He paused to think of just what exactly it was he wanted. ". . . a . . . a form. Yes! That's it! A *form*," he shouted, and almost lost himself in the effort.

"I see," said the air. "But think for a moment. Now you can move freely from the height to the depth, from the length to the breadth. For as it stands, wherever I am, you are."

"Will that no longer be so if I have a form?"

"Well, not necessarily. But it might be more difficult."

"In that case I'll chance it," said Little Breath almost too quickly.

So air made a square and put Little Breath inside it.

the three pieces set before him. Conveying neither pleasure nor disapproval in look or posture, he stood stolidly pensive before his three anxious students.

At precisely this moment, the Master's boisterous wife bullied her way into the room. "I'm hot. I'm tired. And I'm thirsty," she complained. To the startled amazement of all those gathered in the hall, she unceremoniously snatched Allesandro's masterpiece to fill with water to satisfy her thirst. What she lacked in gentility the cup did not, so it broke in her grasp. There was an audible gasp from the onlookers. Yet before anyone could react, she was already filling Massimo's cup. Alas, what this had in strength it lacked in depth, for it was far too shallow to slake such a monumental thirst. She angrily cast the cup to the ground. But it neither broke nor cracked. *"Brutta!"* Massimo muttered, not entirely under his breath. Caring neither for beauty nor for strength, the virago at last grabbed hold of Poverino's cup and drank her fill. She slammed it on the table, chipping its base in the process, and stormed out of the room complaining loudly about the useless gatherings of idle loafers when there was so much work to be done.

There was an awful silence in the hall. The great Master walked silently to the front of the hushed assembly.

"The choice has been made," he said.

"Now you have a form. You are still a part of me, but you have your own unique size and shape."

Little Breath was very excited about his new form. Why, now he was actually distinct. He traveled everywhere throughout the air in his new shape. It should be said, however, that he was not happier than he was before. But neither could it be said that he was less happy than before. He was just as happy, only differently so. Before, he was a happy breath. Now, he was a happy square breath.

One day while wandering contentedly through the air, Square met a triangle.

"I like your shape," said Square.

"I like yours, too," said Triangle.

So Square and Triangle began to go around together. Wherever Square went, Triangle followed. Wherever Triangle ventured, Square tagged along. After a while, they were inseparable.

At last, however, came the dilemma. One day Square said to Triangle, "Wherever you go, I go." Triangle said to Square, "And wherever you are, I am." Then together they said, "Why don't we just fuse into one form!"

Well, that was easier said than done.

"I suppose you'll just have to grow another corner," said Square to Triangle.

"Or I suppose you could drop one of your corners," said Triangle to Square.

"What? And lose one of my most handsome features," he gasped.

"And what would you have me do?" snorted Triangle. "Add to my already unique figure?"

Surely they were at an impasse now. They truly wanted to fuse together, but squares just can't go into triangles, or triangles into squares. No matter how hard they tried, it just wouldn't work.

"What are we to do?" they asked the air after they had become totally exasperated.

"There's only one solution to your dilemma," said the air. He sent over to them a circle.

"But I will have to give up my four corners!" protested Square.

"And me my three!" added Triangle.

There was a long, breathless silence before Circle spoke. "There is no other way," he said.

Square looked longingly at Triangle. "I really do wish to be one with you," he said, "even if I must lose my form."

"And if I must lose my three corners to become one with you, so be it!" said Triangle.

So it happened. The Square inched his way into the Circle. At the same time, the Triangle edged her way into the Circle. When it was over, there was but one Circle.

Suddenly the Circle grew bigger and bigger and bigger, until it stretched as far and as wide, from the height to the depth, of all there was and ever is.

Then one day, in the midst of all this, there came . . . a little breath.

The House

※

More than anything else in the whole world, a man wanted to possess a house of his own. Not just any house, but a house that everyone would marvel at. So he worked long hours and hard days over many years until at last he acquired the house of his dreams.

Alas, once he set foot in his house, he was never seen again. He dared not leave his prize for fear that thieves would steal or vandals ruin what he had labored so hard to possess.

Moral : Whatever you possess, possesses you.

The Waiter and the Captain

※

A ship's waiter, a rather outspoken man not entirely without perception, was annoyed over the excessive attention the diners were giving the impending arrival of the captain.

Wishing to get his goat, one of the diners goaded him, asking, "Well, how do you feel about the prospect of serving the captain?"

"As far as I'm concerned," quipped the waiter, "he is nothing more than our chauffeur."

Moral : Position depends upon perspective.

The San Diego Zoo

※

Among the many marvelous wonders at the San Diego Zoo is the giraffe compound. Enclosed in what is called a natural habitat are several of these magnificent animals. They are every bit as tall and graceful as one might imagine. But they are far more massive and muscular than expected. Tall somehow seems to imply thin. However, these great beasts are anything but skinny. Their necks are thicker and their legs shorter and more powerful than one anticipates. It is not difficult to see why one kick could send an ambitious lion packing.

Yet these massive, stately animals are enclosed in a small compound that seems far too restricting for their size and power. But no cage contains them. There are no bars or walls. There is but a simple, waterless moat, no deeper than the beast's knee, that circles the compound. Freedom is but a mere two steps away.

But they are trapped. All of them are. For not one of them will take the risk of stepping down and across for fear of breaking its neck.

Moral : Fear incarcerates.

The Ice Man

※

A sculptor stood before a great block of ice and decided to chisel a statue out of it. Into every pound of the mallet he put the tortured experience of long years of toil. Into every twist of the chisel there was a grace born of talent and sweat. Slowly, carefully, the figure of a hero emerged. At long last, when the work was done, a monument worthy of acclaim stood before him.

The fruit of the artist serves no other purpose than as gift to another. This labor of love he bequeathed to his son. The son received it with appropriate gratitude, put it somewhere among his goods, and shortly forgot about it.

The ice man melted. The noble, upraised arm became a stump; the muscled torso, a ridged pillar; the strong legs, spindles.

Recalling the love with which his father had bestowed the gift, the son decided to salvage the monument and put his own efforts and talents to bear upon it. After long and hard labor, the ice man reemerged as a magnificent water bird.

Moral : A value cannot be given. It must be acquired.

The Composer

✳

Once upon a time there was a man. A very special man. He was a very special man because he had a very special job. His job was special because he lived at a time when no one else in the whole world had this job. He was a composer.

You don't know what a composer is? He is someone who writes music. You say you know how to write, and I'm sure you do. But composers don't write like the rest of us. We write d-o-g, and that spells dog. And we write c-a-t, and that spells cat. But composers don't write like us. They write *do, re, me, fa, sol, la*. And that spells nothing.

Do, re, me, fa, sol, la. It sounds strange, like a foreign language, doesn't it? As a matter of fact, it's not a foreign language at all, since everybody in the whole world knows it.

What makes it different is that you don't say it, you sing it! Or you can play it. You just can't say it, because when you say it, it makes no sense at all.

Well, one day a *do* was walking around all by himself. He was very happy being a *do*. Everywhere he went people said, "Hello, *do!*" Since he couldn't talk the way we do, he greeted them back by just humming his one note. He loved his note, so he hummed it everywhere. *Huuummmm!* People didn't mind at first, but then he got boring. After all, people get tired of hearing the same note over and over again. But *do* couldn't help it if all he knew was one note. That's all he knew, so that was all he could hum.

It wasn't long before *do* found that life was getting difficult for him. Whenever people got together to talk, *do* would happily join in and hum his one note. Gradually, one by one, the others would leave him until he was humming all by himself. *Huuummm!* This was very discouraging and really unfair. He was sure he had a well-rounded personality. Was it his fault that it was rounded around just one note?

Finally he heard that there was someone who could help him—the Composer. *Do* went to see him.

"Well, my beautiful friend," the Composer said. "I believe I know your problem."

Since *do* couldn't talk like people, he just hummed.

"You're all alone and lonely."

Do hummed excitedly. The Composer was on the right track.

"Well, I know I can help you. But . . ." Here the Composer paused for a long time to show the importance of what he was about to say. ". . . you will have to give yourself up—*completely*—to me!"

Do gasped. How could he give himself up completely to anyone. After all, he was unique. He was special. This demand was unreasonable. Ridiculous! He turned his back and walked away.

So *do* began a solitary trek through life. However,

everywhere he went it was the same. The same old note over and over again. He felt dejected, played out.

He had almost come to the end when the thought occurred to him, "There must be others like me in this world. There just has to be. I must go out and find them."

Thus he began his search. It led him far and wide, but his intuition proved true. He found six others. Only six in the whole world. They were like him, but different. They all knew only one note, but each note was different. He tried over and over to come to accord with them but they were all too individualistic, like himself. He found that *fa* was too flat for his liking. *Ti* was too shrill. And there was no questioning that *mi* was much too self-centered. *Mi* hardly ever listened to him or to any of the others. He found that *sol* was too melancholy, too moody. *La*, on the other hand, was too flighty. Of all the notes, he felt closest to *re*. But somehow even that wasn't consoling. So in the end, *do* came back to himself. Besides, seven was an odd number that needed rounding out.

As a group, they tried pairing themselves off or moving together in threes and fours, but they always ended up at odds with one another. They were each so determinedly individualistic that coming together always resulted in discord.

In total exasperation, *do* shouted out over their noise, "We must do something about this or we shall be lost forever. We must go to the Composer."

"But he demands too much," they argued.

"He wants us to give our all to him," *ti* shrieked.

"Maybe yes. Maybe no," said *la*.

Fa wanted to leave *do* flat. *Re* wanted to side with *do*, but he didn't want to get into it. There was no wondering about who it was that kept shouting, "Oh, *mi!* Oh, *mi!* Oh, *mi!*" Poor *sol* just cried and cried.

"It's either the Composer or oblivion," *do* said.

In the end, he won out. They went over to the Composer as a group.

The Composer arranged them and rearranged them. Over and over again, in different combinations, different groupings. They began to sound harmonious. They began to be melodious. They were orchestrated and rhapsodized. They became . . . music.

One day after performing in concert, the notes sat together for a coffee break. *Do* was feeling especially high, so he broke into a soliloquy.

"I must confess to all of you that at first I was quite terrified about surrendering myself completely. But now I'm eternally grateful that I did. I didn't lose myself as I thought I would. Instead, I feel fulfilled. Somehow I know that this was what was meant for me in the first place."

"Me too," said *mi*.

All the notes laughed together.

The Elephant and the Ant

※

A great elephant made its way to the river to drink. All the animals of the jungle moved aside to let him pass, including the lion, for the mighty elephant is the undisputed lord of the jungle.

An ant stood by the shore of the river wanting to get to the other side. He neither trembled nor moved as the giant approached. When the elephant bent its head, ever so slightly, in order to lower its trunk into the water, the ant accepted the bow and said, "You may take me across the river now!"

The elephant was startled by the command, for no one had ever challenged his authority. Now here was an ant ordering him about as if he were a common slave. It was utter foolishness.

"Why, pray tell me, should I obey you," snickered the elephant.

"Because I am greater than you," replied the ant.

"You, greater than me!" The elephant laughed. "Why, you are smaller than the nail on my littlest toe."

"I am greater than you," the ant repeated imperiously and without humor.

"Tell me why you are greater than me before I stomp

on you and end this discussion," snorted the now angry elephant.

"Stomp as you will," sneered the ant, "for my greatness lies in that very fact. I am immortal!"

"We shall see!" trumpeted the elephant. His foot crashed down again and again, like hammer blows, over the spot where the ant stood. The ant, however, was standing on top of a hole that led deep into the earth, where he sought refuge while the elephant vented its fury.

When the elephant was exhausted and the last of its energy was spent in useless stomping, he lowered his proud head in order to see and enjoy the sight of the dead ant. As he did, the ant emerged from the hole and leaped onto the elephant's trunk.

"I accept your obeisance," the ant sneered condescendingly. "Now take me to the other side of the river."

Thus, through foolishness, the lowly ant became master to the mighty elephant.

The Bridge

※

For an untold number of years a solitary man made his way through an endless desert. He was a traveler with no purpose to his journey and no goal to his wandering. He had all that he could do to just stay alive in that harsh and difficult land. Life had no meaning except for this moving on from place to place in search of food and water.

One day his aimless wandering took him to the edge of a great precipice. This had happened to him before, countless times, whereupon he would simply shrug his shoulders listlessly and turn back. There was no escape from the desert.

However, for some reason this precipice seemed different—unfamiliar. Beyond the cliff stretched a great chasm. Beyond the chasm, off in the distance, was a new land . . . definitely another land . . . a new place. There had never been anything before. Beyond the cliffs before, there had always been endless nothing. This was something new and remarkable. There was actually a place besides the desert!

The man strained to make out as much of this strange land as he could from that distance. He shielded his eyes against the bright glare of the sun and leaned as far out as he could in order to get a better view of it.

What he saw was astounding. It was beyond words . . . beyond mirage . . . beyond imagination. Even from that distance, he could see that the distant land was a paradise. It was everything the desert wasn't. Where the desert was dry and barren, the distant land was lush and green; where the desert was sparse of water, the distant land sparkled with waterfalls and lakes; where the desert offered little food, the distant land abounded with flowers and heavily laden trees. Never in all his years had the man beheld or even dreamed of such a sight.

Now, at last, he found purpose to life. There was a reason to struggle. He must go to that distant land. He must build a bridge.

He hurried back into the desert in search of what he would need to build the bridge. To start, he would need wood. There were trees in the desert—gnarled and scrawny trees, to be sure, but it would be a beginning. Hurriedly, he fashioned himself an axe and set about the task of finding and chopping down trees. The work proceeded slowly, but his spirits were buoyed up with each renewed glance at the distant land. His excitement and enthusiasm sustained him for a very long time, but eventually the immensity of the task bore down upon him.

"I must get help," he said, "or I will never finish the bridge."

There were, indeed, other people living in the desert, but the man had had little commerce with them. Just what was necessary to bargain or to barter and then to move on. Now there would be need of them. Without their help he could never complete the bridge.

He returned to the desert in search of people to help

him. He found a small group of nomads. He described most carefully and in great detail his wondrous discovery. They must come and see for themselves, he told them, if ever there was such a place as this. They followed him to the precipice and saw with their own eyes the marvel that he had described to them.

"Now that we have seen for ourselves and know that this great land is no fable or mirage, we will help you build the bridge," they said, "for we, too, wish to go to that wonderful place."

With more hands set to the task, the work proceeded more rapidly. There was great merriment and spirit among the workers. Slowly but surely, the foundation of the bridge was being set, and the people rejoiced.

But workers must eat, so it was necessary to stop the building for long periods of time while they went out foraging for food. Such delays dampened their enthusiasm and eventually made the task seem interminable.

"We must get help," the man said to the builders.

Back he went into the desert to find those who would act as hunters and farmers to provide food for the builders so they could continue the bridge. These he found, and again he described in the most glowing terms the vision of the distant land and the pressing need to build a bridge. The farmers and hunters and trappers came to the precipice and saw the great sight that had stirred the others and were themselves anxious to join in the effort.

So the builders built and the farmers planted and the hunters brought back game, and the work proceeded. But builders need new tools, farmers new shoes, and hunters new clothes, and thus again the work on the bridge would stop and enthusiasm wane while these new needs waited to be met.

"We must get more help," the man said.

He returned to the desert and brought back with him shoemakers and tailors, carpenters and bakers. These, too, came and saw the great sight and joined their efforts to building the bridge.

So the builders built and the farmers farmed and the hunters hunted, while the shoemakers made shoes and the tailors made clothes and the carpenters made tools and the bakers baked bread, and the work on the bridge proceeded.

All would have continued smoothly and happily except that one day the farmers complained that the shoemakers were not working nearly as hard as they were. The shoemakers said that was because the bread the bakers gave them was not good enough, not even good enough to keep them satisfied and healthy. The bakers claimed that this was because the carpenters made poor equipment for them to work with. The carpenters blamed the tailors, who blamed the hunters, who blamed the builders, who blamed the farmers. The work on the bridge came to a halt. Only the bickering continued, until one by one the different groups began to abandon the project and return to the desert.

"This contention must stop!" the man exclaimed. "They have lost sight of the vision." It was true. As the work progressed, the workers returned to the precipice less and less to refresh themselves for the difficult work they were doing. This must not be allowed to happen again. They must not judge each other's work, only their own. It was true. As the work progressed, it became obvious that some of the workers were stronger than others, more gifted than others, able to do more than others. Comparing had led to contention. Each must do as best he could with what he had, without comparing, and the work could proceed.

So the man called back to the precipice all those who had left, and more. Once again, their hearts were stirred at the sight of the distant land. The man explained his plan to them. All would work together, each according to his own talents and abilities. All would cooperate in the building of the bridge. "And," he concluded, "just so that we will never again lose sight of what we are about, we will all stop working on one day a week and gather here at the precipice to feast our eyes and delight our hearts, to rest and refresh ourselves for the work on the bridge."

The people did as the man suggested, and the work continued. All the people worked together and gathered at the precipice once a week for feasting and rejoicing.

At long last the bridge was completed. The day for the passover to the new land was announced, and the people prepared to celebrate it with great jubilation and solemnity. A procession was organized with the man to lead it. He was followed by singers, who were followed by dancers, who were followed by builders, and so on. The great procession joyfully made its way across the bridge.

When all the people had crossed over to the other side, they discovered that the land was all and more than they had hoped it would be. It was lush and green, with cascading waterfalls and sparkling lakes. There were fields and fields of flowers, and acres and acres of heavily laden fruit trees. It was just as they had seen from a distance. But now they were there.

Yet there was something strange about this new land.

Something odd and unaccountable. The same sentiment had struck them all. They stood there staring at this new land, bewildered by the feeling. What was it?

"I know what it is!" shouted the man. "It's familiar."

He turned around slowly and looked back at the land they had just come from. The others did likewise. To their amazement, the land they had left looked exactly like the one they had just entered.

The Lottery

✳

One day a very fortunate man won the lottery. His excitement could not be contained, the news was so wonderful. His family rejoiced with him, as did his neighbors. His relatives and friends were also very happy for him. Everywhere he went, he told everyone he met of his good fortune.

There was joy and wealth in the lottery that went way beyond his personal needs. More, indeed, than he needed for a lifetime—or many lifetimes, for that matter. Of course, he shared it. First, with his wife and children. Happiness and laughter filled their home. The lottery suddenly opened up new possibilities for them. Wonderful changes began to take place. Without fear about their security, they were able to live freer, less restrictive lives. There was a freedom of style now that definitely had not been there before the lottery. Joy and freedom. That's what the lottery brought them.

But it also brought increasing demands. After the initial excitement passed, there came a steady stream of people who wished to tap into their wealth. Long lost relatives suddenly began to appear. Then came neighbors with sad faces and long stories. The mail was filled with endless requests from countless charities. The telephone rang without stopping, and there was no end to people just dropping in.

After a while it seemed that there wasn't a needy person within fifty miles who hadn't heard about his winning the lottery and didn't want a share in it. First his patience went. Then his benevolence.

"We must leave this place," he told his wife.

"Where will we go?" she asked. "It will all follow us."

"We will go to a new place where no one will know us. We will even change our names. We will tell no one where we are going. And so as not to draw attention once we are there, we will live very frugally. We mustn't display any wealth or even mention the lottery to the children. They are young and I'm sure they will forget about it, especially if we don't show it or talk about it."

"What will we do with it?" his wife asked.

"Bury it, for now. We must live like we don't have it, or it will start all over again. Maybe we can use it in extreme cases as a last resort. But that's all! At least, for now."

So the family moved, and no one knew where they went. The rest happened just as the man said. The wealth from the lottery was buried; the children forgot they ever had it; the parents lived as poorly, if not more so, than their neighbors. They had so managed to put it out of their lives that in time they forgot about it themselves.

When they died, it was all lost. They had even forgotten to leave it as an inheritance for their children.

Moral : Go back and reread the story, substituting the word "Jesus" for "the lottery."

The Sack

※

Once upon a time in a little village set in a valley, there lived a peasant by the name of Joachim. Each day he would leave his meager hut and go about quietly doing his daily chores. But wherever Joachim went he always carried a large sack slung over his shoulder.

It had happened that one day, when he was young, some mischievous boys of the village, like mischievous boys everywhere, taunted him by calling him names. When he retaliated, they did him one better by throwing stones at him. Since they were far too fast and agile for him to catch, he instead picked up all the stones they had thrown and put them into a sack he was carrying. When he got home, he carefully marked the name of each boy on each of the stones. As the days followed and the taunting continued, Joachim diligently collected all the stones and marked them.

Unfortunately, he lived at a time and in a place where everyone was given to throwing sticks and stones. Each time a stone was hurled, whether by a child or an adult, Joachim retrieved it and marked it. Slowly, his collection of stones began to grow.

Because the people of the valley knew what he was

doing, Joachim became concerned that they might steal into his hut while he was away and scatter his stones. So he decided to carry them with him wherever he went. Each day he carried his sack, and each night he marked and sorted the stones. His daily load got heavier and heavier.

One day the king came to the village to appoint a new judge over the people. He chose Joachim. He was to be judge in all matters that pertained to the king and the realm. Dressed in his judicial robes, Joachim sat in judgment over the people of the valley.

Eventually, one by one, they all came before him for judgment. After the charge was read, Joachim reached into his sack and withdrew all the stones with the offender's name written on them. Five stones—five years' imprisonment. Eight stones—eight years in prison. A year for every stone in the sack with your name on it. There were 490 of them in all. Each day there were fewer stones in his sack and fewer people in the village. Unaccountably, however, as the sack got emptier, it never got lighter. In time there were no more stones in the sack, nor people in the valley.

There were no bakers to bake bread or farmers to grow food. No cobblers to make shoes or tailors to sew clothes. There was no one left to talk to or feast with. And there was no revenue for the king.

Joachim had meted out justice. It had given him satisfaction but left him without joy. He was alone and lonely.

At last he decided that he must do something before it was too late. Dressed in his ceremonial robes, he decreed that all the prisoners were to be set free.

The occasion was celebrated with a great feast in the village square. There was eating and drinking and much merriment among the people. Joachim passed freely and happily in their midst, exchanging greetings and well wishes.

Suddenly an angry man who still bore him a grudge shouted a curse at Joachim and followed it with a stone. A hush fell over the throng. Joachim reached down and picked up the stone. Once again, as he had done so many times in the past, he carefully marked it and put it into his sack. Turning slowly, he looked into the eyes of all the villagers. Then he lifted the sack to sling it over his shoulder.

Instead, he began to swing it around and around and around over his head. Finally he hurled it off into the distance. The crowd broke into joyous cheering and shouting.

From that day on, Joachim never carried his sack again. From that day on, there was never any need for him to.

The Box

※

One day a rich man encountered a poor man. He was so excited about the good news he had to tell the poor man that he nearly burst with joy.

"I have such wonderful news for you," he said, his words pouring forth in a flood that could not be contained. "It is a gift! A wonderful gift. A marvelous gift. It is a joy of joys . . . a delight of delights . . . an inexpressible wonder!"

He would have gone on and on, to the dismay of the poor man, except that his excitement about giving the gift overtook his enthusiasm in telling about it. So he abruptly handed the poor man a box.

With his mission accomplished, the rich man unexpectedly hurried off without explanation or elaboration. The poor man looked at the box with more bewilderment than excitement. For it was simply that—a box. It was not ornate or especially attractive. As a matter of fact, it was rather plain and ordinary-looking. The box itself could certainly not have been the reason for the rich man's excitement. It must be what the box contained, the poor man decided as he hurriedly opened it.

The box was empty. There was nothing in it. Nothing at all. It was just a box. The rich man must have been an eccentric. The poor man would have thrown it away, so great was his disappointment, except that he was a practical man and could surely find some use for it. He took the box home with him, stored some loose things he had lying about in it, and put it away.

Some time later while the poor man was wandering about the city, he came upon the rich man once again. The rich man was getting out of the most marvelous late-model car the poor man had ever seen. The rich man recognized him at once and hastened to greet him. He was still unaccountably excited about the box. Not wishing to appear ungrateful, the poor man politely thanked him for the gift but quickly added, "I would be even happier if I had been given a car like the one you have." He was at least honest if not diplomatic.

The rich man was noticeably puzzled by the suggestion.

"But you do have one," he said. He said it so matter-of-factly that it was the poor man who now appeared perplexed.

"I do?" he asked, and gaped mutely at his benefactor.

"Of course you do," the rich man repeated. "It's in the box."

"In the box?" he questioned disbelievingly. "Where? How?"

"Didn't you read the instructions?"

"What instructions? Where?"

"Under the lid. In the pocket under the lid there are instructions. Didn't you see them?"

The fact was that the poor man had been so disappointed at receiving a plain box that apparently was empty that he hadn't examined it at all. He hurried home and retrieved the box.

Sure enough, under the lid there was a pocket and in the pocket a set of instructions. And to add to the poor man's astonishment, the very first instructions were on how to convert the box into a car!

It was not a simple thing to do, but the desire made the effort worth it. At last he had before him a car. It was almost identical to the one the rich man had. He had, indeed, been given a wonderful gift.

The poor man drove his new car everywhere and anywhere he had ever wanted to go. It was a joy beyond telling. For days and months he drove the car, until he became comfortably used to it. Then one day while driving, he chanced upon the rich man once again. This time, however, his benefactor was sporting about in a helicopter.

After a very perfunctory greeting, the poor man remarked at how wonderful it must be to fly wherever you wanted to go. "No need to worry about traffic or even about places a car can't get to," he said. "Now that would be a wonderful gift to have," he added with a twinkle in his eye.

"Why, you already have one," the rich man calmly stated.

"I have a car like yours," the poor man corrected, and quickly added, "for which I am grateful. But I do not have a helicopter."

"This is the car," the rich man said, pointing to the helicopter. "Didn't you read the instructions?"

Truth to be told, the poor man had never read beyond

the instructions for the car, since that was all that interested him at the time.

The instructions for the helicopter were considerably more difficult and involved, but he had resolved to see the task through to its completion. When at long last he did, he had before him a helicopter not unlike that of the rich man.

There was no containing his joy. He flew off at once to the most wonderful and exotic places he had ever dreamed or heard of. The world was, indeed, a wonderful place from the air. It was a feast for the eyes and a banquet for the soul. But it was a meal that left the poor man hungry for the taste of more. He must consult with his benefactor again.

"The car was good," he told him "and the helicopter wonderful. Because of them, my world has grown bigger but so, too, has my appetite. I've seen so many things that I want them all. Would it not be better, then, to have the gift of wealth—like you?"

"You already have the gift of wealth," the rich man said nonchalantly. "It's all there in the instructions."

Once again, the poor man had failed to read beyond his need. This time he resolved to read everything from beginning to end. However, this was a resolution more easily made than kept. The instructions to convert the box into wealth were laboriously lengthy and involved. It would take time and patience, but he knew that the reward was worth it.

Slowly and methodically, he labored over the instructions, doggedly following each procedure as written, painstakingly correcting each miscalculation, until he had successfully converted the box into all manner of remarkable things. It was at one time a house; at another, a yacht; then an airplane; and again a car. As the need occasioned, it seemed that the remarkable box could be molded and shaped accordingly.

One would think that the poor man was happy with this great outpouring of good fortune—and he was. But each possession left him with the anxious desire for another. Alas, the box could be shaped into only one thing at a time, and the instructions were a bother. He no longer had the time or the patience to proceed according to the instructions. He set about on his own to do what he willed with the box. He pushed it, stretched it, molded and squeezed it, to suit his will. It responded as he wished. It became a limousine; then a motor home; then a private jet. He worked harder and more furiously. It became an estate; then a castle. His need became greater still, and so did the objects he craved. It became a building; then a city; then a state. His appetite had become uncontrollable. His effort was monumental. He worked feverishly, without pause, without rest. It was too much. The poor man died.

In the end, they buried him . . . in the box.

But there are two endings to this tale.

. . . Slowly and methodically, he labored over the instructions, doggedly following each procedure as written, painstakingly correcting each miscalculation, until he had successfully converted the box into all manner of remarkable things. It was at one time a house; at another, a yacht; then an airplane; and again a car. As the need occasioned, it seemed that the remarkable box could be molded and shaped accordingly.

His eagerness for more, the poor man kept in check,

never allowing it to outrun or possess him. There was much to gain, and with patience he knew that he could come to possess it all. Over the years his wealth increased and so, too, did his wisdom. In time he was a wealthy and very wise man.

Then one day he came upon a poor man. His affluence and wisdom could no longer be contained. It had to be shared. So he gave to the poor man the best gift that he had to offer—a box!

Moral : The gospel is the good news in a box.

The Thimble

※

One day, after a hard day's work, a thimble got to thinking about itself. "I'm really rather remarkable," he said. "As a matter of fact, I do believe that I'm the greatest thing there is!"

"Not so!" said the bucket. "You are no more than a thimble. I am many times your size. I am the greatest thing there is!"

"Not quite!" said the barrel. "You are no more than a bucket. I am many times your size. I am the greatest thing there is!"

"Hardly!" said the lake. "You are no more than a barrel. There is nothing greater than me!"

"Ha!" said the ocean. "You are merely a lake. There is nothing greater than me!"

"I am greater than you!" said the earth. "I am the greatest thing there is."

"Nonsense!" said the sun. "There is nothing greater than me. I am the greatest!"

"Hogwash!" said the solar system. "You are no more than a Ping-Pong ball in my playground. There is nothing greater than me!"

"I beg your pardon!" said the constellation. "Look at me. Can anything be greater than me?"

"Enough!" rumbled the universe from one end of its infinite vastness to the other until everything, everywhere shook at its voice. Need anything more be said?"

"Yes!" said God to the universe. "You are no more than my thimble!"

The Rich Man and the Beggar

※

One day a rich man encountered a beggar on the street. "Sir, will you give me a coin?" the beggar pleaded.

"I am hungry," the rich man said. "Give me something to eat and I will give you a coin."

"I have no food," the beggar man said, holding out his hands.

"Then give me something to drink and I will give you a coin," the rich man continued.

"I have nothing to drink either," the beggar man said, sighing.

"What do you have in exchange for the coin you want?" the rich man asked.

The poor beggar turned all his pockets inside out and said, "As you can see I have nothing. Nothing at all."

The rich man took pity on the beggar and gave him a hundred silver coins. The poor man was utterly shocked and delighted. He thanked his benefactor profusely and ran off.

Later that evening, the rich man encountered the beggar in the marketplace. The beggar was now dressed in fine new clothes. His face was washed, his hair was combed, and he had a bright, shiny ring on his finger.

"I have come from the square," the rich man said, "where a beggar has asked me for alms for himself, his wife, and his eight children. Give me ten coins from those I gave you so that I might also help him in his need."

"Sir, I have nothing to give," the beggar replied.

"What have you done with the hundred silver coins?" the rich man asked.

"I have spent them all on food and drink and new clothes. Now I have nothing left."

The rich man was deeply saddened. "All that you had was given to you," he said. "Yet you did not follow my example. You have seen only to your own needs. Henceforth, you will always fend for yourself!"

Moral : Greed is its own worst punisher.

Lollipops

※

Once there were two sisters. Each was given a lollipop. Since both of them loved candy, they immediately began licking away at them with great delight.

It wasn't long before Joey happened by. He, too, loved candy, but he had no lollipop.

"Can I have a lick?" he asked Janey.

She really didn't have to think about it at all. "No way!" she said, and began licking all the more furiously. I mean, after all, it was her lollipop, and every lick she gave away meant one less for herself. Let him get his own lollipop.

Joey, however, was never one to be easily put off. So he asked her sister, Julie, "Can I have a lick of your lollipop?"

Now big decisions take time to consider. This was no small matter, to be sure, so Julie had to think about it carefully. After what seemed like an awfully long time to Joey, Julie finally figured it out.

"Sure, you can have a lick," she said, handing him her lollipop.

"You're making a big mistake," Janey warned her sister.

"I don't think so," Julie said, smiling.

"You wait and see. Joey has a big mouth. Pretty soon everybody's going to want a lick." With that said, Janey stuck the whole lollipop into her mouth to protect it against any foreign invaders.

She was right. They did come. First it was Anthony. And then it was Andy and Alice. Julie gave them each a lick. Right after them came Barbara, and Bobby, and Billy. When they left, Charlie, Cindy, and Carol came. Each of them got a lick, and Julie's lollipop quickly began to disappear.

Janey watched all this and began to lick her own lollipop all the more furiously. She kept right up with them, matching them lick for lick.

Then Julie gave a lick each to Darren, Debbie, and Dorothy. Janey took three more licks of her own lollipop. Frankie, Frances, and Freddie got their licks. And Janie took three more again.

Before Julie got to Mary, Margaret, and Mike, her lollipop was gone. So, too, was Janey's.

Both lollipops were gone now. But both girls were still hungry. Of course, Julie was hungrier than Janey.

The next day Joey happened by the two sisters. What do you think Joey had? An ice cream cone!

"Can I have a lick?" Janey asked.

Joey didn't even have to think about it. "No way!" he said.

"Can I have a lick?" Julie asked.

"Sure!" Joey said, handing over his cone. Julie took a lick. True, it wasn't a lollipop, Julie thought, but it was almost just as good. Besides, she liked the change.

When Anthony, Alice, and Andy came by, Julie got a

bite of chocolate, a swig of pop, and a piece of pie. Barbara, Bobby, and Billy gave her a yank of licorice, a ride in a wagon, and three marbles.

Janey cried. She had eaten all that she had and there was nothing left for her now that she was hungry again.

Julie wasn't even up to Darren, Debbie, and Dorothy and she already had more than she knew what to do with. But if she had made it to the Zs that day, she would have found Zachary waiting for her . . . with a lollipop!

Moral : Give and it returns to you a hundredfold.

The Spider, the Bee, and the Caterpillar:

AN ADULT TALE

※

There was atop a rather high bush a solitary blossom of singular beauty. A wandering spider chanced upon it and was so captivated by its splendor that anon he decided to make it his home. But lo, upon reflection he decided that there was richer gain to be had here, so instead, he began to weave a web from leaf to leaf, blocking the passage that was sole access to the prize. "Some foolish and unwary flies, drawn by its sweetness, will surely end up as my supper," he thought. And so it happened.

One day a bee chanced upon the bush. The beauty of the flower and the lure of its perfume were inescapable. But the bee was neither foolish nor unwary. He buzzed angrily in stationary flight pondering his dilemma. This served to signal the spider, who knew at once that here was no mean opponent, so he set out forthwith to reinforce his web.

Into the midst of this conundrum a lowly caterpillar inched its way.

"Buzz off!" warned the bee. "This prize is mine."

"One step closer," cautioned the spider," and it will be your last."

The timid caterpillar was so frightened that she immediately withdrew into herself.

So rests our story, with the reader left to resolve the plot.

The Giant Giant

※

Once upon a time in a forest far away there lived a woodcutter and his son. One should be able to say that they were very happy in their little forest, cutting trees and living simply from day to day, but this was not the case. Alas, the forest they lived in was small, indeed, and all the trees worth cutting were almost all gone. In order to survive, they would have to leave their home and travel to a new forest and begin again. This the woodcutter was reluctant to do, as he dreaded leaving his dear little hut and the quaint little valley he called home. Besides, he was rather old and the trip over the mountain to the next forest was too burdensome a prospect. The days dragged on, with the woodcutter unable to make a decision about what to do.

One day as his son wandered down a forest path, deep in thought about their dilemma, he stumbled upon an old and weatherworn glass bottle. Since the boy was young and still given to flights of fancy, he wondered, if not wished, that perhaps there might be a genie of some sort locked up inside the bottle who would emerge and miraculously solve all their problems. Well, young he may have been, but he wasn't so young as not to know that wishing alone never makes things so. Nervously, with hands trembling, he uncorked the bottle.

The bottle shook violently in his grasp. He threw it to the ground, startled and amazed. The moment it touched the ground the earth shook uncontrollably beneath him. Then a strong wind began to blow out of the neck of the bottle, causing it to spin around and around until a huge whirlwind formed, sucking leaves, branches, and even trees into its terrible vortex. Had the boy not been holding on to a large tree for dear life, he, too, might have been sucked in. Then just as suddenly as it began, everything became calm once again. When the boy looked up, he saw standing there a giant bigger than any he had ever imagined. The giant was so big that he himself was no bigger than the heel on the giant's boot. He wanted desperately to run away, but he was too frightened to move.

Since he wasn't going anywhere, the boy decided that he might as well find out what this was all about.

"Who are you?" he stammered.

"I am a giant, of course," answered the giant.

"Well, you are bigger than any giant I could have imagined," the boy said, trying to reassure himself that this was no figment of his imagination.

"Then you might say that I am a giant giant," the giant said, laughing.

The boy looked at the bottle lying on the ground beneath the giant's feet. Remembering his wish for a genie who could solve all their problems, he asked, "What exactly do you do?"

"I can do all sorts of things," the giant answered, "but if you want to know what I do best, I would say that I stomp and blow best."

"What does that mean?" the boy asked.

"Just what I said. I stomp . . ." At this point the giant lifted one of his huge feet and stomped it on the ground. Then he lifted his other foot and did the same. He repeated this over and over until the ground shook like a violent earthquake. ". . . and I blow," he said, puffing up his cheeks and blowing out a gale of a wind that bent over trees and sent leaves scurrying down the valley and out of sight. "That's what I seem to do best."

"That's all well and good," the boy said, not wishing to offend him. "But that's not exactly what I had in mind."

"What exactly did you have in mind?" the giant asked.

"I'd like you to get rid of that mountain," the boy said. Then, remembering his manners he added, "If you please."

"Whatever for?" the giant asked.

"Well, you see, my father and I have cut just about all the trees we can in this valley and the mountain's in the way of the next valley."

"Then why don't you move to the next valley?"

"Because we don't want to leave our home. With the mountain out of the way, we wouldn't have to," he said, beaming triumphantly at the beauty of his logic.

"Wouldn't you rather have me stomp and blow?" asked the giant. "Think what a hit I'd be with all your friends."

"I'd rather have you get rid of the mountain," the boy repeated.

"That's not as much fun as stomping and blowing. Besides, you'll be disappointed."

"No, I won't."

The giant saw that the boy was adamant. There would be no getting around him. "Don't say I didn't tell you," he said, sighing. He then reached one hand high up into the clouds as if he were grabbing for something. When he brought it down and opened it for the boy to see, there was nothing there. "Look closely," he said. The boy stepped into his hand, searching. Sure enough, lodged in one of the wrinkles was a tiny seed.

"I want you to move a mountain," the boy shouted, "and you give me a seed to start a new forest. What kind of magic is that." Angrily, he tossed the seed aside, picked up the bottle, and corked it once again. He threw the bottle after the seed and returned home.

During the night a heavy rain fell, and the seed began to grow. By morning there stood a tree higher than all the others in the forest. The bottle had lodged in one of its topmost branches and now sparkled in the early sunlight. It caught the eye of a giant eagle, which swooped down and grasped it in one of its claws. On its return flight to its nest the eagle was felled by a hunter's arrow. When the hunter went to retrieve his prize, he discovered the bottle. Without any hesitation, he uncorked it.

Once again the giant emerged, amid trembling earth and violent wind.

"What is it you can do for me?" the huntsman asked, holding the bottle and the cork out for the giant to see, hinting that if he wasn't pleased he could just as easily stop it up again.

"What I do best," the giant said, "is stomp and blow."

"Stomp and blow as much as you wish," the huntsman said, "so long as you bring me wealth."

Immediately, the giant began stomping his huge feet and blowing a mighty wind. In no time at all, wild game of every kind came running past, as well as countless numbers of birds seeking refuge from the wind. The more the giant stomped and blew, the more they came. The huntsman was overwhelmed with game. But there were too many animals and they were coming much too fast for him. Fearing for his life from this incredible stampede, he quickly stopped up the bottle and cast it into the sea.

A wandering fish swallowed the bottle. The fish in turn was caught in the net of a fisherman, who brought the catch to the castle of the king. The royal cook prepared the fish and placed it before the king. When the king cut open the fish, he discovered the bottle.

The giant emerged with his usual fanfare.

"I want power," the king told the giant.

"I want to stomp and blow," the giant told the king.

After a brief demonstration of stomping and blowing, the king called a council of all the rulers of all the kingdoms.

"See now, all you mighty kings and warriors, who defends my realm and gives me power."

The giant stood before the assembled nobles and began stomping and blowing with a power and force hitherto unknown on the face of the earth. All the kings and warriors fled in terror.

"Now I am the undisputed power on earth," the king proclaimed. And so he was. No one dared question the power of the king and his giant. No one dared even approach his castle, so great was the fear of them.

One day the court jester, a dwarf no taller than the king's waist, said to the king, "Oh, great ruler! Does not your power depend upon the giant?"

"It does," the king replied.

"Then if the giant were to be vanquished, your power would end, would it not?"

"It would."

"It seems to me, therefore, that the giant should have a protector. I will be the giant's protector," he said rather pompously.

The king and all his court laughed uproariously at the foolish suggestion of the court jester. The jester, however, did not laugh. Instead, he said, "Come and watch me defend the giant."

The king and his court followed in merry procession behind the jester to the city gate, where the giant stood vigil. The jester stood in front of the giant and proclaimed, "Let everyone heed that I am here to defend the giant against all comers."

The townspeople laughed along with the others over this great foolishness. The king was taking much delight in the charade, so to continue the sport, he asked the jester, "Pray, tell us, what mighty weapon would you use to defend the giant?"

"Why, this pin, of course," he said, extending his weapon for the crowd to see. There was no controlling the laughter now. Everyone from nobleman to serf joined in the hilarity. The jester was well chosen for his profession.

"A worthy weapon," the king announced with mock dignity, "for so worthy a knight. But pray be careful with that noble weapon lest you prick the giant and he flee in terror."

"Sire," said one of the king's barons, "What need have you of the giant if he needs have a protector himself? Let this noble warrior dispatch the giant and take his place as the king's protector."

"So be it!" said the king.

"Yes, so be it!" said the people, laughing.

At that, the jester turned and faced the giant. With one quick thrust, he pricked the giant. At once, air blew out of the giant as out of a great balloon. As the giant diminished, the people gasped in amazement. When it was over the giant was gone—and back into his bottle.

The king decreed that the jester would henceforth be his protector and gave the bottle to the dwarf. Not wanting to be challenged by a return of the giant, the dwarf carried the bottle on horseback up the mountain and dropped it into a fissure where it would be lost forever.

However, a trapper who had wandered into a cave and lost his way chanced upon the bottle. "I wish to be free of this mountain," he said as he unstopped the bottle. As the giant emerged he was too big for the mountain to contain, so it burst asunder until there was nothing left but rubble.

The next morning the woodsman and his son awoke to discover that the mountain was gone. And there, on top of the rubble, was a bottle.

The Clockmaker

✷

In a village high atop a mountain there lived a master clockmaker. All the villagers marveled at the wonderful clocks he made. Not only were they excellent and precise timepieces, they were also masterpieces of art. When the people decided to build a new church, there was no question who should be commissioned to make the tower clock. The great clockmaker decided to put all his talents to the task and make the greatest clock ever.

A large canopy was placed over the tower. The clockmaker worked in secret for many, many months. At long last, the great day of unveiling arrived. The mayor and the townspeople gathered in the square before the church. At exactly noon, the veil fell. The great clock sounded the first gong, and the deep sound of it filled the entire village and was heard even in the valley far below. A door opened at the side of the clockface and a beautiful ballerina emerged. At the sound of the second gong, a stately prince emerged from a door on the other side. As the clock slowly sounded the remainder of the hour, the prince joined the ballerina in front of the clock, where the two danced and whirled together. Above the clockface two doors opened and six musicians dressed in leather shorts and flowered shirts emerged playing their instruments. Everyone delighted over the happy sounds of the bells, chimes, and oompah-pahs that accompanied the dancing figures. When it was over, all the figures returned to their places to await their encore an hour later.

A joyous shout rose from the assembly. Here, indeed, was the greatest clock anyone had ever seen. It was so meticulously planned and so carefully crafted that all agreed it seemed more the work of magic than a craftsman's labor. The great clock became the instant pride of the village.

Each day as the clock struck the hours, the people everywhere would stop what they were doing and look toward the tower. The clock was inerrantly accurate, its movement unfalteringly precise, and the musicians and dancers always in perfect rhythm.

Then one day it erred. For some unexplained reason it had gotten out of synchronization. Everyone, everywhere knew it immediately. As if drawn by some compelling force, all the villagers gathered in the square.

The mayor spoke first. "I have been keeping time for the village for many years. I know about time better than most. I will fix the clock." He then proceeded up the tower. Down below, the people heard banging and clanging—a sure sign that repairs were in progress. Hours later the mayor emerged grease-faced and dishevelled. When the clock struck the hour the ballerina and the prince emerged, but the band did not. The repairs had made things worse.

Now others began to offer their suggestions and to proceed one by one up the tower to make their own corrections. In time the entire movement of the clock was dangerously close to failing altogether.

At last someone shouted above the bickering villagers, "I know who should fix the clock!" A hush fell over the crowd. "Who?" asked the mayor. "Who else but . . . the shoemaker!" the voice announced triumphantly. "The shoemaker is a fine craftsman who plies his trade with diligence and precision. He must be the one to repair the clock!" They all agreed unanimously. The shoemaker was summoned, and he ascended the tower to the cheers of the people. When he returned, the great clock ground to a halt.

Meanwhile, in the master clockmaker's shop the clockmaker worked at his bench as usual. In all the confusion, no one had thought to call for him.

Thoughts

※

Thoughts are like children. They are meant to be seen and not heard.

The Burden

※

Once there was a great and wise king whose kingdom stretched farther and wider than that of any other king and whose authority was total and absolute.

One day a young man committed a serious offense against the king. The opinion of all his advisers was unanimous. For one so lowly to offend against one so mighty, the only just sentence possible was death. So it would have been decreed had it not been for the king's son. He pleaded before the king for leniency and mercy.

"This cannot be," a royal counselor objected. "If such an offense against your august person were to go unpunished, it would be allowing a breach against the order of the realm. To allow one is to allow others. Eventually there would be chaos in the kingdom, and everyone would suffer. For the kingdom to survive, justice must prevail."

"It is so," the others agreed. "The sentence must be death."

"The king's personage is so august," pleaded the son, "that any offense, no matter how small, would have to be punished by death. Eventually there would be no chaos in the kingdom. There would be no kingdom."

Thus the debate raged on, the royal advisers demanding justice, the king's son calling for mercy.

At last the king decided. "The offender must be made to carry a heavy burden up a high mountain. If he survives the ordeal, he shall live."

The royal advisers stormed out of the council chambers in protest against the king's judgment. Had the chaos begun?

Knowing that the load must carry the weight of death, the king's son again intervened. "Royal blood has been offended and only royal blood can pay the price. Justice will be satisfied. I will carry the load," he said.

So the king's son shouldered the heavy burden and began the arduous trek up the steep mountain. In his wake followed the young offender.

The task was, indeed, terrible, for the higher the prince climbed, the heavier the load became. Though he stumbled numerous times along the way, he somehow always managed to rise and continue on again. However, when he was within sight of the top of the mountain he collapsed, too exhausted to continue.

"For there to be peace in the kingdom, the price must be paid," he gasped to the young man. The young man lifted the burden onto his shoulders and carried it the rest of the way to the summit.

The entire kingdom now stretched out before them. With a final effort, the king's son reached down and lifted the load high above his head for the whole world to see.

"It is done," he said, and died.

"Justice is satisfied," said the king, who with his awesome power over life and death then called his son back to life.

"Not yet," said his son come to life again.

"How so?" asked the king.

"Royal blood was helped along the way. Justice demands an equal reward."

"So be it!" decreed the king.

So the prince and the offender lived happily ever after.

The Chocolate Man

✷

Once upon a time there was a chocolate man. He did not know how he became a chocolate man, or when he became a chocolate man, or if he had ever been anything but a chocolate man. The only thing that was indisputable was that he was unquestionably made of chocolate.

As a child he had been told that one of the world's greatest delights was chocolate. To test that knowledge, he decided to eat . . . a toe. After all, a toe is no great loss—and think of the knowledge he would gain, to say nothing of the pleasure. It had proven to be true. Chocolate was truly indescribably delicious. He consumed four toes before he learned to control his appetite by being busy about other things.

By the time he got through adolescence he had eaten his way through his remaining toes, one foot, his left hand and forearm, and two fingers of his right hand. That he made it to adulthood was, indeed, a miracle.

As a man he had managed some mature restraint. Some . . . but, alas, not enough. Was it the delight of the chocolate or the frustration of life that drove him back to himself time and time again? Unfortunately we shall never know, for there was never another chocolate man.

Moral : Self-love is consuming.

Freedom

A boy asked his mentor, "When shall I at last be free?"

"Free," replied the mentor. "Free as what?"

"Free as the birds," replied the child.

"So be it," said the sage, and at once they became birds.

"At last I am free," cried the boy. "Free to soar and fly where I choose, when I choose."

"Not so," replied the birds. "We must follow the wind, for if we stray too far in our migration, we die."

"This is not freedom," cried the boy, following the flock over a forest. "I want to be free."

"Free as what?" asked his mentor.

Looking down at the forest, he saw monkeys frolicking in the bush. "Free as the monkeys to swing from tree to tree as I please, when I please."

"So be it," said the sage. At once they became monkeys.

"Now, at last, I'm free," cried the boy as he swung from tree to tree.

"Not so," said the monkeys. "We must never stray too far or apart from one another lest we become food for predators."

"This is not freedom," cried the boy. "I want to be free."

"Free as what?" asked his mentor.

"The lion is the king of the jungle," replied the boy. "Free as the lions to roam where I please and eat when I please."

"So be it," said the sage. At once they were lions.

"At last I'm free," cried the boy, roaming the jungle as the king of beasts.

"Not so," said the lions. "We must follow the herds or we will not eat. Nor may we stray beyond our limits, or we will be prey for man."

"This is not freedom," cried the boy. "I want to be free."

"Free as what?" asked his mentor patiently.

"Free as man to do as I please, when I please."

"So be it," said the sage. At once they were men.

"Now, for sure, I'm free," said the boy turned man.

"Not so," said his wife. "There are chores to be done, children to be fed, obligations to be met."

"This is not freedom," cried the boy. "I want to be free."

"So be it," said the sage, and at once he became a child again.

Moral : Freedom is where you make it.

The Teacher, the Artist, and the Child

※

A wise man stood before an assembly of people and presented to them this parable.

"A teacher and an artist were once involved in a mighty dispute over who had greater influence in the world. In order to settle the issue, they decided that they would each put the full weight of their talent to bear upon a child. It was agreed that the teacher would teach the child the essentials of reading, writing, and arithmetic so that he might be able to carry on commerce and become a success in the world. The artist would teach the child to recognize and appreciate beauty. At last the time came for the child to enter the world on his own.

"To prove who had the greater influence on the child, both the teacher and the artist were allowed to offer one final suggestion for the child to remember them by.

"I have taught you what you need to be a success in life," the teacher said, "so every time you deal with money, think of me."

"I have taught you the beauty there is in life," said the artist, "so every time you see a rainbow, think of me."

"Whom do you suppose the child will think of more?" the wise man asked the crowd.

Without hesitation, they exclaimed, "The teacher!"

"The child learned better than you," said the wise man, "for he saw that money was just one color of the rainbow."

The Castle

※

Once upon a time there was a wonderful prince. He lived in a valley where he was loved by all the people. He and his people worked together, ate together, and celebrated together. There was great peace and harmony in the land because of the love they all had for one another.

One day the people decided to show their great admiration for the kindly prince.

"Let us build him a castle," they said. "A fine home for him to live in, even better than those of other princes."

"Together we will build the most wonderful castle the world has ever seen," they exclaimed, "for with our prince we are beyond doubt the happiest people on earth."

It did, indeed, turn out to be the most marvelous castle imaginable. The walls were hewn from rare marble, so fine as to be almost transparent. The towers were made from precious stones—one of ruby, one of sapphire, one of emerald, and one of onyx. The floor was inlaid ivory and the roof gold. People everywhere agreed that it rivaled the sun in brilliance and beauty.

Word of the castle began to spread beyond the valley. At first the curious came from nearby. Then travelers began arriving from far and wide. It became necessary for the villagers to set up inns and restaurants to provide for the needs of these tourists. The greater the influx of travelers, the greater became the commerce in the village.

The villagers knew that their good fortune was due to the wonderful castle. In order to assure their continued prosperity, they would regularly polish its stones and clean its towers. The castle continued to sparkle like a jewel, drawing visitors from the world around.

The village grew into a city. There was commerce and industry. But with the trade came rivalry, with rivalry jealousy, with jealousy hate, and with hate contention. There was no longer peace in the valley.

Finally, one day the wonderful prince emerged from the castle. The people had all but forgotten that he lived there. Without saying a word, the prince walked around the castle seven times. When he was done, the castle collapsed.

"Why have you done this?" the angry people shouted.

"I have done nothing," the prince replied. "Seven times I walked its circumference searching for your image in its walls and on its towers. I found none. The castle no longer reflected the hearts of the people. It could stand no longer."

Moral : When love ends, so does the structure built by it.

The Maybe Miracle

※

A crippled and blind beggar slowly and painfully made his way toward the town of Capernaum. He groaned in agony with each passing step. The pain was alleviated somewhat when he leaned heavily on his crutch and took the pressure off his feet, but it returned with punishing intensity when he used the crutch to sweep the road ahead of him for obstacles. Hope lay before him in the city people called "his city." Jesus the healer was to be found there.

At the city gate the beggar approached the elders for help.

"Is it true that Jesus-bar-Joseph can be found here?" he asked.

"It is true," they replied.

"Is it true that he is the worker of miracles that I have heard so many speak of?"

"He has performed many wondrous deeds," they replied.

"Is it true that he has made the blind see and the crippled walk?"

"I myself have seen him make a clay with his spittle and rub it into a blind man's eyes and he could see again," one elder commented. "And I," said another, "saw him stretch out his hand to a man crippled from his youth and raise him to his feet." "These deeds and others like them he has done here in Capernaum and elsewhere we hear tell," said the oldest of them.

"You are the elders who sit in judgment for this town, are you not?" the beggar continued. "Tell me how it is that he can do these things?"

"It is in the touch," one said, and the others readily concurred, showing that the matter had already been carefully deliberated and decided upon. "Power goes forth from his touch. If you would have him heal you, make sure that he touches you."

These last words the beggar repeated over and over to himself as he winced his way into town. As he approached the square, he heard the commotion of an assembled crowd. It took only a moment to discover that Jesus was there. He cried out, "Jesus-bar-Joseph, have pity on me!" There was no response, so great was the din of the crowd. So he called out all the louder, "Jesus, son of David, have pity on me."

"Who is it that calls out to me?" Jesus asked. The crowd grew silent. It was the rabbi's time to teach, not to perform works. They were annoyed at the disturbance.

Someone led the beggar forward.

Jesus noticed that despite his stooped body and pain-wrenched face, the beggar was not as old as he appeared. "What is it you want of me?" he asked.

"Lord, I can barely walk. My feet are in constant pain."

Jesus looked down at the man's feet. "Is it any wonder you are in pain?" was his astonishing reply. "You are wearing your left shoe on your right foot, and your right shoe on your left foot. How did this come to be?"

"Lord," he replied, "when I was of the age to wear shoes and was given a pair, I simply put one on one foot and the other on the other foot. Since that time I have always put the same shoe on the same foot. I have always done it that way."

"If you wish to walk without pain," Jesus said, "change your shoes around."

This the beggar did, and at once he could walk again. Why, he even jumped up and down in painless delight. But before Jesus could go on again, he called out once more, "Jesus, son of Abraham, have pity on me!"

"What is it you want of me now?" Jesus asked patiently.

"Lord, that I might see again."

Jesus looked closely at the beggar's eyes. They were covered with clay. "Who did that to you?" he asked.

"As a child, I once peeked into the house of the local physician to see him at his work. He discovered me and scolded me, putting this paste over my eyes, and warned me that if I were ever to remove it I would go blind."

"He was an evil man," Jesus said, "but there is no reason for you to go about blind because of his sin. Go and wash it off."

The town fountain was but a few steps away in the center of the square, so the beggar immediately did what Jesus told him. When he washed away the mud he could see again. It was wonderful.

No longer in pain when he walked and able to see where he was going, the beggar also lost the appearance of a doddering old man. He was young and sprightly as befitted his years. He skipped his way along through the town gates. The elders stopped him in his exodus.

"We see you got your miracle," they commented.

"Yes! A miracle!" the young man replied.

"Tell us," they queried, "was it in his touch?"

"Oh, my!" he exclaimed. "I knew there was something I forgot to ask him to do."

The Peddler

※

Once upon a time there were two kings. The king of the North ruled over a kingdom that was cold, barren, and poor. It had practically nothing positive to speak of except water, and that it had in abundance. The king of the South, on the other hand, ruled over a kingdom that was almost the opposite. It was hot, verdant, and the people fared well. But there was never enough to drink.

The kingdoms were situated on two plateaus with a valley between them. But it might as well have been a bottomless pit, because no one ever passed from one kingdom to the other except a peddler. He crossed it frequently as he went from one to the other barking his wares.

I have pots. I have pans.
I have hammers and saws and tools of every kind.
I sell anything and everything.
But wisdom I give away free.

One day the king of the North asked the peddler, "Is it true that the kingdom of the South has more than enough to eat?"

"So it has been said," replied the peddler.

"Then I must make war on them, for we have barely enough to survive on. Have you bows and arrows for me to buy?"

"I have bows and I have arrows to sell," said the peddler. "But wisdom I give away free."

"I have no need of wisdom for now," shouted the king. "I need implements of war."

So the king bought a plentiful supply of bows and arrows, and diligently trained his people for war. When at last he judged them ready for battle, he approached the peddler for advice.

"What wisdom can you give me now that we are ready for battle?" he asked.

"You will win with water," was the peddler's strange reply.

The king laughed at him. "That is not wisdom, that is foolishness!" he said.

"Water is precious," said the peddler.

"Well, if it *is* so precious," snorted the king, "then I shall pay you with water." So he did, and with his army he set off for battle.

The war between the two kingdoms raged, but too long for the king of the North and his men, for their bodies were weak from lack of food. They returned home unvictorious.

Not long after the battle, the peddler entered the kingdom of the South.

I have pots. I have pans.
I have hammers and saws and tools of every kind.
I sell anything and everything.
But wisdom I give away free.

The king of the South had the peddler brought to him. "I hear tell that in the kingdom of the North there is an abundance of water," he said.

"So it has been said," replied the peddler.

"Then I must go and take it," shouted the king, "for my people have barely enough to live on. Have you bows and arrows to sell so that I can make war against them?"

"I have bows and arrows in abundance to sell, but wisdom I give away free."

"I have no need of your wisdom now, peddler, but for your arms so that I can prepare my people for war."

So it was that for many months the king of the South prepared his men for war. When at last they were ready, he called the peddler to seek his advice. "What wisdom do you have for me before we go into battle?" he asked.

"You will fare well with food," answered the peddler.

At this the king burst into laughter. "Food enough we have, and then some. But what good is food without drink?"

"Food is precious," the peddler replied.

"If it *is* so precious, then I shall pay you with food," he said, laughing.

Once again the two kingdoms engaged in war, and once again neither king emerged victorious. This time the soldiers of the South could not sustain the battle because they were too weak from thirst.

But alas the die was cast, and the desire of each for what the other had could not be quelled. Emissaries were sent between the two kings, and a war to the finish was agreed upon.

When the fateful day arrived, the kings led their armies to the very brow of their plateaus. The soldiers stood row after row in awesome battle array. At the sound of the trumpet blast, the first wave scurried down the hill to the valley below.

Just as they were about to begin the battle, the peddler emerged from seemingly out of nowhere.

I have pots. I have pans.
I have hammers and saws and tools of every kind.
I sell anything and everything.
But food and drink I give away free.

Before the startled eyes of the hungry and thirsty soldiers, the peddler laid open his cart filled with the food and drink the kings had supplied him with. Without hesitation, the soldiers threw down their arms so that they could feast on the bounty before them. Without thought of war or danger, they sat side by side eating and drinking their fill.

From atop the plateau, the kings eagerly watched the battle below. It seemed that the first wave of men had all been felled because they were all on the ground. The command was given, and the next wave descended. When these arrived and saw the feasting, they, too, joined the others. The battle appeared to be proceeding faster and fiercer than either king had expected. Two more rows were sent charging into the valley. They, too, discovered that there was food and drink aplenty since the kings had been most generous in paying the peddler.

Then another most strange thing began to happen. The soldiers of the North, where it was cold, were dressed in the flimsiest of clothes. This was because it was too cold to grow much food, so there were precious few animals for wool or skins. But the soldiers of the South, where it was warm, were dressed in heavy clothes because the sun made the animals' hides thick and their fur dense. One moment they were eating side by side together, and the next, they were exchanging clothes.

Report of these strange occurrences was carried back to the kings. They became furious and set out at once to straighten matters out.

They were appalled by what they saw. Not one man had been slain. Not one arrow had been shot. Not only were they not fighting one another, some of them were actually—*napping!* This was preposterous, and the kings chided their soldiers in no uncertain terms. The king of the North grabbed hold of one of his soldiers and throttled him.

"Take your bow and shoot that man!" he commanded.

"Excuse me, sir. But I'm not one of your soldiers," he replied.

"Then what are you doing dressed in our uniform?"

"We switched," answered the man. The king of the North was apoplectic with rage.

The poor king of the South was faring no better. "How can we fight one another when we don't know who's who?" he screamed. "This is preposterous! Who is at the root of this fiasco?"

"The peddler," they replied, pointing to where he stood in their midst. Then, in uncontrollable fury, the two kings rushed over to the peddler and struck him down.

"Now that he's dead, maybe we can get on with this war," they said. Then, in order to straighten things out, they ordered their men to exchange their clothes again and return to their own sides.

While the men were sorting themselves out, the peddler suddenly rose to his feet and began to assist them. The soldiers were awestruck! Was he a ghost? How did he do that? Those nearest him asked him. He leaned over and whispered something to them. Before long, the other soldiers noticed that the peddler was alive again. Instead of returning to their waiting armies, they stayed to ask the peddler themselves. To them, too, he whispered his secret.

When the kings returned to their respective sides, they expected their wayward soldiers to be following immediately behind them. When they turned and saw them still in the valley talking to their enemies, there was no placating them.

"Kill them all!" they commanded. After all, you can't have a war if your soldiers are eating and drinking and exchanging clothes with one another. These men had all been contaminated, so it was best to just get rid of them and start over fresh.

The next wave of soldiers from both sides rushed into the valley and began killing all those who had remained below. But before the slaughter was finished, those who had been slain first got up and began to help those who were slain after them. This time both kings had accompanied their troops into battle just to make sure that there would be no more foul-ups. If they had not seen it with their own eyes, they would never have believed it. Word was spreading among the troops like wildfire. There was whispering everywhere.

The two kings became hysterical with rage. *"Enemies don't whisper into each other's ears!"* they shouted.

The situation was definitely getting out of hand. It was all the peddler's fault. They were so mad they could kill him. But they had already done that. Well, then, they were so mad that they could kill their soldiers for listening to him. But they had done that, too. Well, they were so mad that they could kill each other. But not before they found out what it was the peddler was telling everybody. They were mad, but not stupid.

So the peddler whispered in each of their ears the wisdom he had told the others.

"Ridiculous!" said the king of the North.

"Foolishness!" said the king of the South.

So the two kings went off—alone, since none of their subjects would follow them. One went to the East, and the other to the West—to get as far away from this wretched valley as they could and to try all over again. As they wandered off into the horizon, the peddler packed up his cart and followed behind them, saying:

I have pots. I have pans.
I have hammers and saws and tools of every kind.
I sell anything and everything.
But wisdom I give away free.

This tale, I suppose, is not complete until you know the wisdom the peddler whispered to those who would listen. But I give you fair warning, if you don't want people to think you foolish or ridiculous, you had better whisper it to one another. The peddler's secret is: *Love One Another!*

The King and
His Three Servants

❈

I

Once there was a great and powerful king. He called
one of his servants into his throne room.

"What is it you wish of me, sire?" the servant asked.

"The people of the kingdom of the North have need of
me. Go to them and see to their needs."

"Is there anything my lord wants me to take with me
for the task?" the servant asked.

"There is," the king said, and went off to his treasure
room. When he returned, he gave to his servant a package. The servant took the package and set out immediately to do his king's will.

When he arrived at the northern kingdom, the servant
traveled throughout the land to see for himself what might
be the cause of the people's difficulty. What he saw confused and distressed him. The land was rich enough, but
very little of it was being used for farming. The homes
everywhere were broken, charred and ramshackle, but
no effort had been made to repair them. The people
themselves were the worst of all. They were skinny and
drawn, poorly dressed and in a constant state of anxiety.
There was no accounting for this strange state of affairs
judging from the promise that the land held out and the

potential inherent in the people. So the servant called a meeting of the people of the land.

"Why is it that you have not farmed this rich land? Why are you living in such squalor? What is it you people are so anxious about and fearful of?" His questions were more a demand or a reprimand than a query.

"To answer the latter will explain the former," a spokesman volunteered, since there was apparently no governor or mayor or local ruler among these strange people.

"We are afraid because of our enemies."

"Explain this," the servant demanded.

"Beyond the pass," he said, pointing to a narrow opening between two high pillars of mountains, "our enemy lives and bides his time waiting for us to prosper. When we farm the land to surplus and our granaries are full to overflowing, when we fix up our homes so that they sparkle with beauty, they ride through the pass to plunder and pillage. They carry off all that we have worked for and destroy what they cannot take. For us to prosper is to invite disaster."

"To live in fear is a greater disaster," the king's servant said. "You must first do something about your enemy."

"It is no use," the people replied. "We are weak and they are strong. If we farm any more than just enough to survive, they know what we are about and they set upon us. As we are, we cannot withstand them."

"The question does not take great pondering," the servant replied. "We must block the pass."

"This, too, has been tried, but to no avail. Nothing can hold them back," complained the people.

"Nothing but the mountain itself," the servant shouted

triumphantly. There lay, not too far from the pass, a huge boulder that could, indeed, hinder any army's passage into the valley. That is, if it could be moved to the proper place.

"We have tried. It can't be done," the people cried.

The servant wished to see for himself. So all the men of the kingdom came forth to push against the mighty stone. But all their combined strength could not so much as budge it from its resting place.

"We are too weak and it is too strong," the people announced.

There was no solution. There was no hope for this pitiable kingdom unless the king's servant could find the answer in the package the king had given him. But what possible remedy could be found in so small a package? Was there magic here? Was this some sort of wizard's box?

With flying, impatient hands the servant hurriedly undid the package. Beneath the wrapping was . . . a book.

Now this was a strange gift, since the king's servant could neither read nor write. But he was no fool. "If the body is too weak, then the king must want us to make the mind strong. I must learn to read," he said.

So he did. And as he did, he learned great and marvelous wisdom from the book. When at last he had learned all that the book could teach him, he was ready to take on the great task for which he had been sent.

"We must move the stone," he ordered. And none too soon, for rumor had it that the people of the kingdom were about to undergo another siege.

"Tell us how we can move it." the people said.

Through the most marvelous arrangement of pulleys and levers and hoists, they lifted the boulder onto several carts tied together. However, to their dismay they discovered that as big as the stone was, it was not big enough to block the passage or severely deter an onrushing army.

There was no time to lose now, for spies of the enemy had reported what the people of the valley were doing and the enemy was assembling its forces for an attack. A new plan had to be devised, and quickly.

The servant pondered the dilemma for a while and then decided. "We must create an avalanche," he said.

There was a plateau about halfway up the mountain, just high enough for a stone that size to cause an avalanche of sufficient size to block the pass. So every beast, man, woman and child pushed, pulled, and struggled with every ounce of their strength until the stone had been successfully hauled up the mountain. And none too soon, for below them, the enemy army had just entered the far end of the pass. There wasn't a moment to lose.

There was no time to assemble a hoist to get the stone off the carts. They had brought the load just so close to the precipice when those pulling had to withdraw. The task was too great for those pushing. The servant had to think and think fast if he was going to save the day. His newly acquired knowledge was being put to the ultimate test.

"Knock out the front wheels," he ordered. The men hammered away at the wheels until they broke off. The carts tilted down, causing the boulder to slide off with just enough momentum to continue rolling down the incline and over the cliff. On its way down it seemed to take with it half the mountain. When the dust settled, there was no longer a pass between the mountains.

The people cheered and cheered.

"That should put a stop to them," the servant shouted. "And if they decide to try to come over the mountain to attack us, the effort will severely weaken them. By that time we will have built ourselves up, and we'll be strong and they will no longer be a problem.

"Hooray for the king's servant," the people shouted.

"And for the king and his wonderful package," the servant replied.

II

In the meantime, the king called in another servant.

"What is it you wish of me, my lord?" the servant asked.

"My people in the kingdom of the South have need of me. Go to the kingdom and see to their needs," he ordered.

"This I will do, your majesty. Is there anything I should take with me?"

Once again, the king entered his storehouse and returned with something for his servant. He had placed on the floor before him a large wooden chest. "You may have need of this," the king said.

The servant left at once for the southern kingdom. When he arrived there he, too, made a survey of the land and the people. The land, he found, was rocky and barren. Precious little of it had been cultivated for crops. The people were weak and drawn. It took no great intelligence to deduce that this was the result of not enough farming. Indeed, the only thing in the kingdom that appeared to fare well were the magnificent wild horses that abounded everywhere.

"Why are you people so emaciated and weak? Why have you not prepared more land for farming?" he asked.

The spokesman for the people stepped forward. "To answer the latter is to explain the former," he said. "We have not cultivated more land because, as you can see, the ground is very rocky and resists our weak efforts at pulling the plow. We farm little, so we eat little. We are barely strong enough to plow what we need to survive."

"You pull the plows?" the servant asked, bewildered. "Why do you pull the plows when there are horses here strong enough to pull a thousand plows?"

"As you have said, the horses are strong but we are not. They are strong and wild, and we are too weak to break them. They have thwarted all our efforts to subdue them."

"This cannot be," the servant shouted. "I myself will break them, and you may harness them for plowing."

While the people watched, the servant made his way toward a group of horses. They were neither frightened nor intimidated by his approach. In fact, they seemed defiant. In a quick movement that caught the horse and the crowd by surprise, the servant leapt atop one of the marvelous beasts. With two powerful kicks, the horse sent the man flying unceremoniously to the ground.

Undaunted, the servant tried again, and again almost effortlessly the horse bucked and reared and unseated him. The servant tried another horse, with the same catastrophic result. The people laughed good-humoredly at his obstinacy. It was all to no avail. Not one of the beasts was he able to break, in spite of hours of trying. If he with his strength was unable to subdue even one of them, could he expect these weakened people to do better? It was all but hopeless. Unless the chest the king had given him contained some magical answer.

When he opened the chest, the king's servant was surprised to find inside all manner of exercise equipment—barbells, dumbbells, stretch springs, and so on. The people were puzzled at the sight of these things. Not so the servant.

"I am strong," he said. "But not strong enough, it seems."

So the king's servant took to exercising each day and for long hours throughout the day. Gradually his muscles got bigger and he grew stronger. Week after week, month after month, he continued his strenuous routine until he felt as strong as the fabled Hercules himself.

"I am ready now," he told the people. Again he set off for the horses. This time he went looking for an especially strong one—the leader of the herd. When he found him, he jumped astride the defiant stallion before it could even snort a challenge. They were off, with the horse bucking, jumping, kicking, and rearing for all it was worth. But no amount of effort could unseat its rider. They were at it for hours, but the servant yielded not an inch. At long last, the horse tired. The servant had matched his strength against the horse's and won. The horse was broken.

"Harness him to a plow," the servant ordered triumphantly, and set off for the next horse.

"Hooray for the king's servant," the people shouted.

"And for the king and his marvelous chest," the servant shouted back.

III

In the meantime, the king called in a third servant.

"What is it I can do for my lord?" the servant asked.

"In the kingdom of the west my people have need of me. Go see my people," said the king.

"This I will do as you wish. Is there anything the king would have me take along for the task?" the servant asked.

"There is," said the king, who left the room and shortly returned with his son. "Take my son with you," he said.

When the servant arrived at the western kingdom, he, too, made a long and extensive survey of the place and its people. The land was a good land, pleasant to behold and suitable for farming. There was also enough wildlife for hunting and trapping. The problem here was the people. They were a sorry lot if there ever was one. They were crude and argumentative. They were loud, rough, and physical. They fought with each other so constantly that wars were commonplace. Those who were not battle-torn and scarred were sick and diseased. They stole from one another, lied to one another, and abused one another in whatever way possible. The king's servant was totally dismayed over what he found there.

More than anything else, the servant wanted to please the king. The reports that had come back to the castle about what the other servants had done only stirred his desire to do as well, or better, than they. Now here he was with no less than the king's son himself to watch him and report back to his father about his accomplishments, and he was at a total loss over what to do? How was this going to look to the king's son? What report would he send back to his father?

Finally it occurred to him. Since the others had done so well with their tasks, he would go first and learn from them. Then he would be in a better position to know what to do with these sick and rebellious people.

Thus he journeyed to the kingdom of the North. There

he discovered the need for intelligence and wisdom. At the kingdom of the South, he learned of the need for strength. Wisdom and strength were the keys to success in the other kingdoms. He must use those keys to solve the problems of the kingdom of the West.

Wisdom told him that he would need an army to subdue these quarrelsome people. Strength told him that it would have to be a very strong army.

So he set about his task. He chose those with promise of intelligence and made them officers in his army. He chose those with promise of strength and made them his warriors. These chosen ones he taught and trained himself, until they were ready to go forth and pacify the land.

IV

At last the king said, "I must go now and visit my servants to see what they have done with my lands and my people."

When he arrived at the kingdom of the North, he found a people well educated and prosperous. There was no longer fear and anxiety in the land.

"Well done!" said the king to his servant. "Because you have done well with what I have given you, I give you this land and its people as my gift. Do well and prosper."

When the king arrived at the kingdom of the South, he found a ruddy and healthy people, strong and able-bodied. The fields abounded with good, rich food.

"Well done!" said the king to his servant. "Because you have done well with what I have given you, I give you this land and its people as my gift. Do well and prosper."

When the king arrived at the kingdom of the West, he found strife and contention everywhere. There was no peace, no prosperity. The people were still poor and sick. There had been no relief.

"What have you done?" the king asked his servant.

"I have gone and learned wisdom from your servant in the North and strength from your servant in the South. I have used this knowledge and strength to build an army that will keep these rebellious people subdued. Through intelligence and strength I wished to bring peace to this land."

"Have you done it?" the king asked.

"Not yet," the servant replied. "They are a difficult people, and perhaps we are not yet intelligent enough or strong enough to accomplish our goal."

"See now, my servant, that you have not done what was yours to do. Nor were you able to use the gifts given to the other servants, for they were given for their purpose and not yours. Tell me, what does your wisdom say to this—can one gain peace by making war?"

"I don't see how, your majesty, when you put it that way."

"Tell me, too, has your strength made the weak strong?"

"No," your majesty.

"Now tell me, what have you done with my son?"

"Your son, my lord?" the servant questioned. "What have I done with your son? Well, I had hoped to impress him. To show him what I was going to accomplish for you."

"But what have you done *with* him?" the king asked again with emphasis.

"Why, what does he do?" the servant asked.

"Ask him," the king replied.

The servant turned to the king's son. "What is it you can do?" he asked.

Without saying a word, the king's son walked out into the midst of the people. He saw among them a blind man. He reached out and touched him. At once the man could see. Lying on the ground was a lame man. He took him by the hand, and the man stood up. He was crippled no longer. He continued moving among the crowd. He who was deaf, or mute, or sick he healed. When at last he spoke, his very utterances brought peace to the hearts of all who heard him.

"I didn't know!" the servant screamed out. "I didn't know."

"Because you did not use what was given to you, I will take this land and these people away from you."

"What will become of this kingdom, then?" the servant asked.

"I will leave it for my son," the king replied.

The Sage and the Puppet

✳

Once upon a time there was a great wise man. People came from far and wide to consult with him about their problems and to learn from his wisdom.

One day a foolish young man came to the sage and asked him, "Great master, what must I do to gain perfect wisdom?"

Without the slightest hesitation, the wise man drew out a puppet and placed it on his lap. "Whenever I have a problem," he said, "I ask my puppet for the answer."

"But . . ." replied the young man, "the puppet can say only what you think."

"Ah!" exclaimed the sage, "You have discovered the secret to perfect wisdom."

Moral : A man who has himself for an adviser has a fool for a counselor.

Heredity

❋

The mule is a very stubborn animal. It comes from mating a donkey with a mare. I suppose if I had an ass for a father and a horse for a mother I'd be stubborn, too.

The Hunting Dog

※

A man wanted a pet dog. To be his pet the dog had to be the right size, the right color, and the right shape. He found just the dog he was looking for. It was a hunting dog. It made no difference that the man wasn't a hunter. It was the right animal for him.

The man loved the dog as much as any man could love his pet. He fed it, nurtured it, pet it, loved it. The dog never lacked for food or comfort. The man never lacked for a trusty and loyal companion.

At times the dog seemed restless, unfulfilled. When the man threw a ball, the animal was confused between pointing and fetching. When walking through fields the dog would stray, sniffing frantically, searching confusedly. In the end he would return to his master's side, accepting a pat on the head in compensation.

The dog grew old comfortably and died. The man mourned the loss of a wonderful companion. The dog never knew the thrill for which it was born.

Moral : One who settles for contentment may lose fulfillment.

The Most Agreeable Kingdom

❋

Once upon a time there was a most agreeable kingdom. All the people everywhere agreed about everything. If the sun was shining and the weather was pleasant, everyone agreed that it was a pleasant day. If it was raining and cold, they all agreed that it was a terrible day. They agreed that when the sun rose in the morning it was time to get up, and when it went down in the evening it was time to go to bed. Everyone worked at the same time, ate at the same time, and played at the same time. This was most agreeable, because if everyone is eating at the same time, no one will interrupt your dinner. If everyone works at the same time, then no one can waste your time. Even when it was time to play, the people would break into groups and do whatever each group had agreed upon. Yes, all in all it was a most agreeable kingdom.

Now if you think that trouble is going to come to this kingdom, it's only because you must be one of those people who can't leave well enough alone.

Well, that's exactly what happened when You came into the kingdom. It was certainly pleasant enough at first, but You got a little itchy and restless. When You wanted to sleep late some mornings, everyone agreed that You should get up like all the rest. When You didn't want to work, everyone agreed that You had to work. You thought, "Well, at least when it comes time to play, I won't play with anyone." But even here that didn't work, because they put You into a group with people who agreed that they didn't want to play. You couldn't even have a bad day, because when You felt disagreeable, You was put into a group with others who were disagreeable and they all agreed. What was You going to do?

Now if you're thinking that there must be a way out of this, that's just like You.

Well, You decided to go and see the king. But You couldn't go until others agreed to go along. You see, You can't do anything in the agreeable kingdom unless others agree with you. So You decided to play a game called Go and See the King, and when others agreed to play with You, You got what You wanted. You was so clever. But You always knew that.

When You stood before the king, You should have been agreeable like everyone else in the kingdom, but instead You said, "I've got a bone to pick with you." Well, the king was not going to be disagreeable, certainly not in the Most Agreeable Kingdom, so he agreed with You and said, "I've got a bone to pick with You."

Now if you think this story is getting ridiculous, then you agree with You, who said, "Now this is ridiculous!"

"Why?" asked the king. "Why shouldn't people everywhere agree with you? It makes for a most agreeable kingdom."

To be honest with you, You couldn't think of an answer. So the wise king continued.

"Do you want to be disagreeable?"

"No," You said.

"Do you want others to be disagreeable?"

"No," You said.

"Then what's ridiculous?" asked the king. The argument had come full circle in only two questions. Now that was pretty clever when You came to think of it. You wanted to be disagreeable and in two seconds flat You had to agree with the king.

"How did you do it?" You asked.

"I didn't," said the king, smiling agreeably. "You did."

Well, if you think this story is getting confusing, we had better let the king explain.

"You see," he said, "there is a secret I learned a long time ago when this was a most disagreeable kingdom. At that time no one anywhere agreed with anyone. Now no king wants to rule over such a kingdom, but I was at a loss over what to do about it. So I took my problem to the great Rorrim for a solution. 'Come back in three days' time,' I was told, and I did what I was told. The wizard handed over to me a chest and said, 'Henceforth, whenever anyone disagrees with you, go secretly to your room and open this chest. Herein lies the solution to every problem you will ever face.' Well, I took the chest back to my castle and have since learned all my great wisdom from it. I have modeled my kingdom on the wisdom I have learned from the secret of the chest."

"May I see it?" You asked.

Down to his very soul, the king was confounded by the request. A secret is not a secret once it is told. But the king could not be the king of The Most Agreeable Kingdom if he refused. You had outdone the king, and with only one question! You would have to be shown the secret of the chest.

The king led You up a dark staircase to a locked room at the top of the castle tower. He dragged the chest over to the window so that You could see what was inside.

"You open it!" You said, trembling nervously.

"I agree," said the king, who stepped aside and waited for You to open the chest.

You decided to open it rather than belabor the point. With shaking fingers, You slowly lifted the heavy lid.

Suddenly the room was flooded with a blinding light. You staggered back, almost blinded.

"It's light! It's light!" You shouted. "The secret of the chest is light!"

"Look again," the king said.

You approached the chest cautiously. You squinted and with eyes almost closed peered inside.

At the bottom of the chest was . . . a mirror.

"It is the wisdom of the ages," the king said, closing the chest so that You could see once more.

Well, that is the story of The Most Agreeable Kingdom and the secret of the chest and the wisdom it teaches. Now you know what to do whenever someone disagrees with you. You do what You always does. But you always knew that, didn't you?

The Tower

※

Once upon a time there was a king. "I want to build a tower," he said. So he called in all his counselors.

"It must be made of stone," some of them suggested. "It must be massive and strong so as to show the king's strength."

"It must be made of wood," offered the others, "so that it can be ornate and decorative to show the king's good taste."

"Stone!" shouted the former.

"Wood!" bellowed the others.

Alas! The poor king was unable to decide which was better, for each had its merits. In the end, he decided that they should use both.

The solution was not as happy as it at first seemed. His advisers could never seem to agree on which should go where. Should the foundation be of stone? Should the facade be of wood? What should the stairs be made of? The counselors bickered endlessly. The work progressed slowly. The king cried despairingly, "Will no one help me?"

No one dared speak. After all, not even the king's renowned counselors could agree. No one, that is, except the court jester.

"Why do you want to build a tower?" he asked.

"Why? Why?" stammered the king. "What a foolish question!"

"Why, indeed!" repeated his advisers. "Such a foolish question."

Undaunted, the jester repeated his question. "Why do you want to build a tower?"

The king became furious. "Why?" he shouted in rage. "Why, but to reach the sun, of course!"

"Of course?" said the counselors. "Yes, of course! Why else?"

Before the court jester could utter another word, the king's advisers had already embarked upon a new course of action.

"If the king wishes to reach the sun, then perhaps wings would be a better solution," one of the sages suggested.

"Not wings!" interrupted another, "for the king might tire before he reaches it. Better he should be shot from a cannon."

"No! A cannon will not get him far enough," argued yet another. "I have a far better solution. A hot-air balloon. As hot air rises, so will your majesty, all the way to the sun."

The bickering began all over again, each one repeating the merits of his own suggestion.

In desperation the king shouted out again, "Will no one help me?"

When the din abated, it was the court jester who spoke up again. "Why does the king wish to go to the sun?" he asked.

"Why? Why, indeed!" raged the king.

"Yes! Why, indeed!" repeated his counselors.

"Why?" shrugged the jester.

"Why? I'll tell you why!" shouted the king. "Because I'm afraid of the dark. That's why!"

A deep and profound hush came over the assembly. The silence said it. There was nothing that could be done. Night was night, and there was no getting away from it. People were supposed to sleep at night. That's what it was for. They must resume the tower.

Just then, the court jester did the strangest thing. He took a burning branch from the fire and held it aloft. "Here, now, is your sun," he said to the king. "Take it with you wherever you go."

Thus fire, which heretofore had been used only for heating and cooking, was for the first time used for light. From a lowly court jester the king learned a valuable lesson: It is better to light a candle than to build a tower.

The Falcon and the Crutch

※

I

Once upon a time when falconry was king and all the noblemen of Europe indulged in the sport, the king of France gave to his son, on his seventh birthday, his very own baby falcon. Now this was an unusual gift for a child because as everyone knows, falcons can be dangerous. But the king felt that if the two were to grow up together, they would become the best of companions. The prince fed his pet and took care of it quite responsibly. The young man so wanted to please his father and grow up to be exactly like the king. He could hardly contain his joy the day he took the bird out for its first hunt. Would he be successful? Would the falcon fly off and never return once it realized it was free? Off the boy went with the king and his noble barons, each with his own magnificent bird, each bird wearing the colors of its master's house.

The royal hounds raced wildly through an open field, scaring up partridge everywhere. There was no longer time to think or worry, the sport was on. The prince let his falcon fly. The air was filled with the screech of birds and the excited shouts and hurrahs of the noblemen. Before long, the birds began to return with their captured prizes. During the frenzy of activity, the prince had lost sight of his bird. As the masterful hunters arrived one by one, he saw that his was not yet among them. He looked anxiously to the sky. The king saw his apprehension but said nothing. This was the sport of men. The others had all returned, each triumphant with its prey clutched in the unshakable grasp of its strong talons. But not the prince's. The sky was empty, as was his heart. There was merriment and banter, but the prince stood off by himself searching the heavens. When the others took notice of him, they looked to their liege and smiled knowingly. There was silence. Tears welled up in the young prince's eyes. Just when it seemed that all was lost, he heard the faint, familiar shriek of his peregrine. From behind some tall trees at the edge of the forest where it had wandered off, the magnificent young bird emerged. In its claws was a young partridge.

It was a great day. The prince would often recall the pleasant memory of the noblemen teasing him about the size of his first catch, and the backslappings of approval. He knew that the future would bring even better fortune.

And so it did. His falcon became the best hunter in the realm. He was so proud of his bird that he had taken to walking around all day with it clutching firmly to his forearm. It was almost an effort for him to put the bird aside for the night, so attached to each other had the two of them become.

Alas came the fateful day when a great fire destroyed the royal hunting preserve. There was no prey anywhere for the falcon to hunt. The prince took the bird out each day, but they returned empty. It was then that the bird began to nip at its master's arm in frustration. It was annoying at first; then a serious nuisance; and finally a painful and continuous bother. He tried leaving the bird in a cage, something he had never done before. But, somehow, without that beautiful plumed appendage he had carried around with him for so long, he felt naked. Nor did the bird sit quietly in its cage. Unused to such imprisonment, it shrieked and squawked constantly. Feeling he had no other alternative, the prince set the great bird free.

The bird flew off and circled the castle. Its keen eyes searched the near and far horizon. Then, with an awful shriek, it swooped down in pursuit. It flew straight down toward the castle and through a window into the room where the prince was standing. The bird's cry startled all those in the room, including the prince. It flew straight to the prince and perched on his forearm. It looked directly into the prince's eyes. It was understood. This was where it belonged, and the prince had to accept it.

From that day on, the prince carried the falcon everywhere and always.

II

Once upon a time there was a most beautiful princess. She was all that the king and queen could ever hope for in a child. She was a treasure in both beauty and disposition.

Alas, as if by some evil design, or by the curse of some wicked witch, or perhaps merely by some unfortunate happenstance, the young princess was thrown by her pony and left crippled. She would never again be able to walk without a crutch.

She grew up as all children do. Her beauty never diminished, but the same could not be said of her disposition. The crutch was always with her both physically and mentally. Even though the other inhabitants of the castle court had long since ceased to take notice of her condition—for in truth, there were so many other preoccupations to take up their time and thoughts—the princess could not or would not forget it. She complained about her plight regularly and frequently. Even when she said nothing, she somehow managed to make her condition apparent to those around her. Now it must be said that the people of the realm were sympathetic and at times understanding, but there was nothing they could do for her. Unless, perhaps, she were to marry. After all, when princesses marry they do tend to live happily ever after.

So the king announced to the princess and the kingdom that a match had been arranged. The news, however, distressed the princess beyond telling. Who could possibly want to marry her? Would he be marrying her out of pity? Even though all marriages were arranged in those days, she was convinced that hers had to be. It could not be otherwise. She was unconsolable.

Preparations for the royal wedding were a continuing agony. Would no one save her from her misery?

As the day drew nearer, the poor princess grew more frantic. She desperately wanted to cancel or at least postpone the wedding, but the king would not hear of it. It was decreed, and his word was as irrevocable as was her crutch.

But as fate can sometimes seem cruel, it can also just as unexpectedly be quite generous. An itinerant knight, hearing of the princess's plight, revealed to her the most wonderful news. There was in the neighboring kingdom a wonderful witch who could perform the most marvelous good works. She could unquestionably heal the princess, for he himself had seen her do that and more.

Without telling a soul about her happy discovery, the princess set off in haste to find the wonderful witch. The task was easier than she had expected, as there were many others in pilgrimage to the same place.

Leaning even more heavily than before on her crutch, she anxiously entered the witch's hovel. Without any ado or fanfare, the witch took some powder from one of her many jars and sprinkled it on the hapless girl. "You no longer need that crutch," she said quite simply. That was all there was to it. The princess let the crutch fall to her feet. It was true. She could stand without it. She no longer needed it. That which had been her life's companion was no longer necessary.

"You may leave now," the witch said. "There are others waiting." The princess was more puzzled than relieved.

At long last the great nuptial day arrived. The castle church was filled with invited guests from both kingdoms. The organ bellowed the entrance of the princess. All eyes turned to the bridal procession. At the end of the entourage was the princess all dressed in white. She hobbled down the aisle, leaning on her crutch for support. She made her way down the aisle most slowly and solemnly until she stood before the bishop. From the apse to her side emerged the prince. He, too, made his way slowly and most solemnly to his awaiting bride. Clutching tightly to his forearm was a large falcon.

The princess and the prince were married that day, and all people everywhere agreed that the two of them were made for each other.

A Strange and Special Christmas

A SCREENPLAY FOR TELEVISION

❊

The setting is the living room of an extremely wealthy home. An undecorated Christmas tree has just been placed on a stand near a blazing hearth. A wealthy boy (girl) of about twelve is seated snugly on a sofa paging casually through a Christmas catalog. The boy's father, tastefully dressed in a business suit, enters the room and gazes at the tree.

FATHER: Now that's a fine tree.

[The boy pays no attention to the remark at all. He looks at his father curiously.]

FATHER: What are you doing, Chris?

CHRIS: *[Without looking up.]* I'm just looking through this catalog to see what I want for Christmas.

FATHER: Is that so?

CHRIS: *[Matter-of-factly.]* Yes. There are so many things I want for Christmas, I may as well get it out of the way right now.

FATHER: Well, it seems to me there's more to Christmas than just getting what you want.

CHRIS: I suppose.

FATHER: Not everyone has what we have, you know. Besides, you have so much already.

CHRIS: But there are a lot of things that I don't have yet, and Christmas is a good time to get them. I've only just begun and already there are things here that I just gotta have. *[He continues paging through the catalog slowly, as if not wanting to miss a thing.]*

FATHER: You're missing the point, Chris. *[He pauses, looking at his son, who has ceased to pay attention to him. Chris continues to turn the pages. His father waits a moment longer, then walks away. Chris continues paging through the catalog until he dozes off.*

Standing in the place where the father was is a man in costume. It is the father in disguise. He is now the Magic Wish Man. *The tree in the room is now fully decorated.]*

MAGIC WISH MAN: *[Coughs loudly.]*

CHRIS: *[Wakes up and looks startled.]* Who are you?

MAGIC WISH MAN: I'm the Magic Wish Man. Who are you?

CHRIS: I'm Chris.

MAGIC WISH MAN: Well, why did you send for me?

CHRIS: I didn't send for you!

MAGIC WISH MAN: You must have. I always come at Christmastime to children who are in need.

CHRIS: Well, I don't need you. I always get whatever I want for Christmas.

MAGIC WISH MAN: I see. *[Rubbing his beard pensively.]* This is 43 Crescent Parkway, isn't it?

CHRIS: Yes.

MAGIC WISH MAN: Are there any other children living here?

CHRIS: No.

MAGIC WISH MAN: Then I must be here for you.

CHRIS: That's ridiculous. I told you, I always get what I want for Christmas. I just tell my parents and what they don't get me, somebody else does. My aunts or uncles or somebody.

MAGIC WISH MAN: This certainly poses a problem. This couldn't be a mistake. They don't make mistakes up there (pointing up). There must be a need here somewhere. *[He looks around the room and settles on the tree.]* Oh, yes. I see. *[He mumbles half aloud.]* You seem to be an intelligent boy. Do you see anything missing about this tree?

CHRIS: *[Gets up and walks over to tree and gives it a quick once over.]* Yes. There's no star on top.

MAGIC WISH MAN: Well, fancy that. You are a clever boy, indeed. *[Mumbling and rubbing his beard.]* Now why wouldn't there be a star there, do you suppose?

CHRIS: I'm sure I don't know. It wasn't even decorated a minute ago.

MAGIC WISH MAN: *[Ignoring the comment.]* The tree needs a star. If there's no star, there can be no gifts.

CHRIS: What's that supposed to mean?

MAGIC WISH MAN: Oh, that's simple. The wise men brought the first Christmas gifts when they followed the star. If there's no star, how can there be gifts?

CHRIS: That's ridiculous.

MAGIC WISH MAN: If it is, then tell me, where are the wise men? *[He points beneath the tree.]*

CHRIS: *[Down on his knees looking at the crèche. All the figures are there except the Magi.]* I'll be. You're right. There are no wise men. *[Pauses, thinking.]* Does that mean I really won't get what I want this Christmas?

MAGIC WISH MAN: Well, I am the Magic Wish Man, am I

not? I should be able to do something about this. Tell me what you wanted for Christmas.

CHRIS: *[Paging frantically through the catalog.]* There's a book here. It says here that it is one of the best stories ever written. And it has a superspecial surprise ending. I love books like that, and I really want this one for Christmas.

MAGIC WISH MAN: Remember, there's no star up there, so I'm not really sure how this is going to work out. *[He reaches into his pocket and comes up with a fistful of magic dust.]* Well, here goes. *[He throws the dust into the air above* Chris. *There is a puff of smoke.]*

The scene is a different place, a sparsely furnished living room. Chris *walks around the room. There is no one there. He shrugs and sits down on a worn-out sofa to read his book. The title is* The Prince and the Pauper. *When he opens to the first page there is nothing written there. There are just bumps. He goes through page after page, but it's the same thing. In frustration he closes the book and slams it on his knee. A girl appears, standing behind another easy chair and leaning over the top of it.*

GIRL: Are you having trouble?

CHRIS: *[Looks at her curiously.]* Yes. I got this book that I wanted to read real bad, but somebody goofed. There's no writing in it.

GIRL: *[Laughing.]* You must have picked up one of our books.

CHRIS: What's that supposed to mean?

GIRL: It means you can't read it unless you can read braille.

CHRIS: I can read very well, thank you. Even if I can't

read another language, there's no writing on any of the pages.

GIRL: Braille isn't another language. It's English. Only it's written in bumps.

CHRIS: That's ridiculous.

GIRL: Well, do you see any bumps on the pages?

CHRIS: *[Looking closely.]* Yes, there are? What is it, some kind of secret code?

GIRL: Not exactly. It's written for blind people.

CHRIS: For blind people? You mean blind people can read?

GIRL: Of course, we can.

CHRIS: Are you blind?

GIRL: Yes, I am.

CHRIS: *[Momentarily confounded.]* Well, the Magic Wish Man said that he wasn't . . .

GIRL: The who?

CHRIS: The Magic Wish Man.

GIRL: Don't be ridiculous.

CHRIS: Well, whoever he was, he told me that he wasn't sure how things would work out and he really goofed. He gives me a book I'm dying to read, only now I can't read it.

GIRL: But I can.

CHRIS: I don't need any help.

GIRL: *[Moving around the chair to the couch.]* Good, then you can read it to me. I just love stories.

CHRIS: But I can't read bumps.

GIRL: Braille.

CHRIS: All right, braille. But I still can't read it.

GIRL: Then you do need help. That's all right. I'll read it to you. *[Before he can object, she extends her hand for the book. He gives it to her. She begins.]* The Prince and the Pauper. *[Sound fades. She is no longer seen. Just her voice is heard saying in conclusion . . .]* . . . and they all lived happily ever after. *[Just her hand is seen giving Chris back the book.]*

CHRIS: That was a good story.

MAGIC WISH MAN: I thought you'd like it.

[Chris *looks around. He is back in his own chair. The book has changed back to the catalog.]*

MAGIC WISH MAN: Was there something else you needed for Christmas?

CHRIS: Oh no, you don't. I don't want to go through that again. That wish got all goofed up.

MAGIC WISH MAN: We must have done something right. There's one wise man at the stable.

CHRIS: *[Sees that one Magi presenting a gift is before the crib.]* Well, I'll be. But I don't care. I don't trust these mixed-up gifts.

MAGIC WISH MAN: If that's what you want, it's all right with me. Only remember, if there's no star there'll be no gifts for Christmas. None at all.

CHRIS: But I gotta have gifts. There are still a lot of things I want. Like . . . like . . . *[Turning pages.]* Like these moon boots.

MAGIC WISH MAN: Moon boots it is. *[He reaches for his magic dust and throws it.]* Here goes again.

Chris *finds himself standing at one end of a gym. There are children playing at the other end. He looks down at his feet. He is wearing a pair of beautiful moon boots.*

CHRIS: All right! Now that's more like it. They're beautiful. Wait till everybody sees them. Nobody in school will have a pair this nice or this expensive. Just wait till they see them. *[He goes to move, but he is unable to. His feet seem stuck to the ground. He tries to lift his leg, but it won't budge. He tries the other leg with the same result. He struggles frantically for a while. A boy standing nearby leaning on parallel bars calls to him.]*

BOY: You must be new here.

CHRIS: Who are you?

BOY: My name's Tom. What's yours?

CHRIS: I'm Chris.

TOM: Whatcha doin'?

CHRIS: I'm trying to move, is what I'm doing.

TOM: *[Laughing.]* That's what we're all trying to do.

CHRIS: You don't understand. I got these beautiful moon boots, but I can't seem to move.

TOM: All dressed up and no place to go, eh?

CHRIS: This isn't funny. How am I going to show off these boots when I can't move my feet.

TOM: That's no big deal. We all have that problem. It just takes a little help getting started.

CHRIS: I don't need any help.

TOM: Suit yourself. You'll learn eventually, just like the rest of us.

CHRIS: I'll just get my feet out of these boots. They're too heavy, that's all. *[He struggles to get out of them, but to no avail.]* That Magic Wish Man goofed it again.

TOM: What are you talking about?

CHRIS: Oh, nothing. All I wanted to do was show everybody these boots I got for Christmas. Now I can't.

TOM: Sure you can. Let me show you. *[He reaches down and picks up a pair of crutches.]* Look. Take these and put them under your arms like this. *[Demonstrating.]*

Then go and show off your boots. *[He leans back on the bars and slides the crutches over.*

Chris *looks reluctant at first, but the sounds of merriment coming from the other end of the gym stir him. He reaches down and tries the crutches. He drags his feet but manages to go a few yards. When he tries to hurry, he stumbles.]*

TOM: Here. Throw them back to me. Let me show you how to do it. [Chris *slides them back, and* Tom *joins him.*]

CHRIS: It's no use. *[He is standing on his feet again.]* This is ridiculous.

TOM: What's ridiculous is you standing there and you won't let anyone help you.

CHRIS: I should be helping you, not you helping me.

TOM: Here we all help each other, kid. Now do you want to get around or not?

CHRIS: I do.

TOM: OK, then. *[He calls out.]* Joey! Bring my friend some wheels. *[A boy in a wheelchair comes, pushing another wheelchair in front of him.]* Here! [Tom *pushes it to* Chris.] Take a load off your feet.

[The three of them fade down to the other end of the gym. Laughter and kidding. Camera eventually zeroes in on Chris *laughing.]*

CHRIS: This is great. *[He lifts up both feet, looking at the boots. Suddenly he's back at home sitting on the couch with his feet extended.]*

MAGIC WISH MAN: Beats me what you kids see in those things. They look too heavy to get around in, if you ask me.

CHRIS: *[Checking to make sure of where he is.]* I don't think I'm going to ask you for anything anymore.

MAGIC WISH MAN: Why not? There's a second wise man at the stable. Don't you think it's worth another try to get the star. You seem to be doing OK at it thus far.

CHRIS: You mean, if we get it right one more time I get what I want for Christmas.

MAGIC WISH MAN: I thought you were getting what you wanted.

CHRIS: I'm not sure.

MAGIC WISH MAN: Then it seems to me you ought to try one more time. What else did you want?

CHRIS: [Paging through the catalog.] Here's a good one. A foos ball game. If I had my own game, I could practice and beat every kid in school.

MAGIC WISH MAN: One foos ball game, coming up. [POOF!]

Chris *again finds himself in strange surroundings. This time it is a group home for the retarded. Before him is the brand-new foos ball game he wanted. There's no one around, so he begins playing by himself. However, he soon discovers that it is not a game that can be played alone.*

CHRIS: I can't play this by myself. I gotta have somebody else to play against. [At this moment a retarded boy enters the room.]

BOY: Hi!

CHRIS: [Looking suspiciously. The boy is a Mongoloid.] Hi.

BOY: What's that?

CHRIS: It's a foos ball game. [The boy comes over without being asked and starts turning the knobs. Chris stands watching him, his hands on his hips.] That's not the way to do it. Let me show you. [They play for a while, *but* Chris *gets exasperated trying to show him what to do.]* No! You don't know what you're doing. Isn't there anybody else here I can play with?

[Looking hurt, the boy walks out. A whole group of retarded people come in and try it. All to no avail.]

CHRIS: This is the Magic Wish Man's worst goof-up of all. These people can't do anything right. *[He goes over to a chair and puts his head in his hands.]* Now what am I gonna do until this is over?

[The first boy comes back and taps him on the shoulder. Chris looks up. The boy extends his hand. Chris takes it and the boy leads him outside. Once outside, the boy starts to make a snowman. Eventually Chris joins in. The two of them get into it. The others come out and join them. By the time they're finished and the snowman gets his hat and pipe, they are all laughing and having a good time.]

CHRIS: This was fun. *[He no sooner says this than he gets hit with a snowball. He reaches down to make a snowball and the foos ball falls down in front of him. He picks it up and stares at it. He is back at home again, standing before the Christmas tree. His father walks into the room.]*

FATHER: Well, I see the tree's decorated. Nice job. Is it all finished?

CHRIS: I'll tell you in a minute. *[He gets down on his knees and checks the crèche. There are now three wise men.]* Yes. It's all finished.

FATHER: But there's no star on the tree.

CHRIS: *[He looks up to make sure. There is no star. He looks momentarily puzzled. Then he looks down at his hand. The foos ball is gone. In its place, there's a star.]* Yes, there is. It's right here in my hand, Dad!

[The scene ends with the three handicapped children, dressed as the wise men, presenting gifts of gold, frankincense, and myrrh. The camera rises to the sky above them, where a star is shining brightly.]
Finis!